PRAYING
WITH
ANGELS

About Richard Webster

Author of over seventy-five books, Richard Webster is one of New Zealand's most prolific authors. His best-selling books include *Spirit Guides and Angel Guardians* and *Creative Visualization for Beginners*, and he is the author of *Soul Mates, Is Your Pet Psychic?, Practical Guide to Past-Life Memories, Astral Travel for Beginners, Miracles*, and the four-book series on archangels *Michael, Gabriel, Raphael,* and *Uriel*.

A noted psychic, Richard is a member of the National Guild of Hypnotherapists (USA), Association of Professional Hypnotherapists and Parapsychologists (UK), International Registry of Professional Hypnotherapists (Canada), and the Psychotherapy and Hypnotherapy Institute of New Zealand. When not touring, he resides in New Zealand with his wife and family.

PRAYING
WITH
ANGELS

RICHARD WEBSTER

Llewellyn Publications
Woodbury, Minnesota

First Edition
First Printing, 2007

Book design by Steffani Chambers
Editing by Brett Fechheimer
Cover art © 2007 by Photodisk
Cover design by Gavin Dayton Duffy
Llewellyn is a registered trademark of Llewellyn Worldwide, Ltd.

Library of Congress Cataloging-in-Publication Data
Webster, Richard, 1946–
  Praying with angels / Richard Webster. —1st ed.
      p. cm.
  Includes bibliographical references and index.
  ISBN-13: 978-0-7387-1098-3
  ISBN-10: 0-7387-1098-9
  I. Angels. 2. Prayer. 3. Spiritual life. I. Title.
  BL477.W43 2007
  202'.15—dc22
                                                    2007006589

Llewellyn Worldwide does not participate in, endorse, or have any authority or responsibility concerning private business transactions between our authors and the public.

All mail addressed to the author is forwarded but the publisher cannot, unless specifically instructed by the author, give out an address or phone number.

Any Internet references contained in this work are current at publication time, but the publisher cannot guarantee that a specific location will continue to be maintained. Please refer to the publisher's website for links to authors' websites and other sources.

Llewellyn Publications
A Division of Llewellyn Worldwide, Ltd.
2143 Wooddale Drive, Dept. 0-7387-1098-9
Woodbury, Minnesota 55125-2989, U.S.A.
www.llewellyn.com
Printed in the United States of America

Other Books by Richard Webster

To Write to the Author

If you wish to contact the author or would like more information about this book, please write to the author in care of Llewellyn Worldwide and we will forward your request. Both the author and publisher appreciate hearing from you and learning of your enjoyment of this book and how it has helped you. Llewellyn Worldwide cannot guarantee that every letter written to the author can be answered, but all will be forwarded. Please write to:

Richard Webster
℅ Llewellyn Worldwide
2143 Wooddale Drive, Dept. 0-7387-1098-9
Woodbury, MN 55125-2989, U.S.A.

Please enclose a self-addressed stamped envelope for reply,
or $1.00 to cover costs. If outside U.S.A., enclose
international postal reply coupon.

Many of Llewellyn's authors have websites with additional information and resources. For more information, please visit our website at http://www.llewellyn.com.

❧ Contents

For my older son,
Nigel

Up the Hammers!

Introduction

Angels are beings of light. The word *angel* comes from the Greek word *angelos*, which means "messenger." This is because the main task of angels is to carry messages to and from God. Angels also provide help and comfort whenever necessary.

As angels are believed to have been created on the second day of Creation, it's not surprising that angels predate history. Many primitive religions believed in beings that were able to cross from the physical world to the kingdom of the gods. Zoroastrianism, the religion founded by the Persian prophet Zoroaster (sixth century BCE) contained a form of angel known as *amesha spentas*, the holy immortals.

The angels of Judaism came originally from the cosmology created by Zoroaster and, later on, Christian angels were based on the Hebrew tradition. Still later, the Christian and Jewish angels had an influence in the angelology of Islam.

Angels are mentioned on numerous occasions in the religious books of Judaism, Christianity, and Islam. In fact, many of the most important occurrences in all of these faiths took place with the help of angels. These religions have differing views on the nature and duties of angels, but they all implicitly accept the reality of them.

However, throughout history there have also been people who have refused to accept the possibility of angels. One person who thought a great deal about the subject was Alfred Russel Wallace (1823–1913), the Welsh naturalist, who devised a theory of evolution by natural selection that was published at the same time as that of Charles Darwin. He wrote: "If, as I contend, we are forced to the assumption of an infinite God . . . it seems only logical to assume that the vast, the infinite chasm between ourselves and the Deity is to some extent occupied by an almost infinite series of grades of beings, each successive grade having higher and higher powers in regard to the origination, the development, and the control of the universe."[1]

---

1. Alfred Russel Wallace, *The World of Life* (London: Chapman and Hall, Limited, 1910), 392.

This is a logical argument, as every organization of any size has a hierarchical structure. It's not too far-fetched to believe a similar structure—a hierarchy of angels—is maintaining the entire universe.

Only a few years ago, people were embarrassed to talk about angels. In 1943, when Dr. Mortimer Adler wanted to include an article on angels in a proposed book on the great ideas of Western civilization, he received strong opposition from his editorial committee.[2] Fortunately, he persisted, and the article was included. In 1975, when Billy Graham's book *Angels: God's Secret Agents* appeared, it was one of the few books available on the subject. Today there are hundreds, reflecting people's renewed interest in this ancient topic.

It is also possible that angels have started taking a more active interest in mankind, too. I hope this is the case, as we need them more than ever in the world we live in today.

There is no doubt that you can communicate with angels. The more open you are to the possibility of angelic contact, the more likely you will be to experience the joy and exhilaration of these remarkable manifestations. You need to be alert, open, and ready to experience angelic contact.

The best way to approach this book is to read it through first, deciding on the topics that interest you most. Work with these first, and after you have achieved some success with them, move on to explore some of the other chapters. Everyone is

---

2.   John Ronner, with Sr. Fran Gangloff, *The Angel Calendar Book* (Murfreesboro, TN: Mamre Press, 2000), 173.

different, and subjects that fascinate you will not necessarily appeal to someone else. Start by performing the rituals in the way I have described them, but then use your intuition to change anything you feel necessary to make the rituals entirely your own. By doing so, you will develop in your own way and may make discoveries that help other people establish their own personal connections with the angels.

Over the years, I have seen the astonishing results people have achieved by communicating with angels through ritual and prayer, and I hope this book will help you, too, to establish a relationship with God through His angels.

Prayer

The word *prayer* comes from two Latin words: *precarious*, which means "obtained by begging," and *precari*, which means "to beseech or implore." Consequently, prayer has always been used to ask for something for yourself or for others.

Although few people discuss prayer in everyday conversation, praying is an extremely common practice. A Gallup poll revealed that ninety percent of the United States population prays, and sixty percent of these people considered prayer to be an extremely important part of their lives.[3]

Prayer is a spiritual communication with God, the architect of the universe, whoever or however you conceive of God. Prayer is a deliberate act that enables you to experience the sacred and communicate with the universal life force. Clement of Alexandria (c. 150–c. 215), a theologian and early Christian father, said: "Prayer is conversation with God." Prayer affirms your connection with the divine.

Anyone can communicate with God through prayer. It makes no difference who you are. You can belong to any religion, or none. Prayer is not reserved for any specific faith or religion. It makes no difference if you are rich or poor, good or bad, black or white. Different people express themselves in varying ways, but it makes no difference how you phrase your prayers.

Language skills are irrelevant. Jesus taught: "Your Father knoweth what things ye have need of, before ye ask him" (Matthew 6:8). A delightful Hasidic tale tells of a man who wanted to pray, but had left his prayer book at home. He decided to recite the alphabet five times, and allow God to rearrange the letters to form the required prayer. God replied, "Of all the prayers I have heard today, this one was the best because it came from a simple and sincere heart."[4]

A silent prayer in which the person communes with the divine can be as effective as any other form of prayer. Consequently,

---

3. Margaret Poloma and George Gallup, *Varieties of Prayer* (Harrisburg, PA: Trinity Press, 1991), ix.

4. Anthony de Mello, S.J., *Taking Flight* (New York: Doubleday, 1990), 22.

everyone has the ability to communicate, and establish a relationship, with the divine. Saint Teresa of Ávila, the sixteenth-century Spanish mystic, expressed how sublime this form of communication was when she described it as "an intimate friendship, a frequent conversation held alone with the Beloved."[5]

The desire to communicate with a higher power is universal. Thousands of years ago, the psalmist described this need using the analogy of a deer longing for water. "As the hart panteth after the water brooks, so panteth my soul after thee, O God. My soul thirsteth for God, for the living God" (Psalm 42:1–2). In other words, our souls are constantly striving to reach a spiritual level, and prayer is the most natural way to achieve this.

There are many different types of prayer. You can praise God. You can give thanks to God. You can request healing for yourself and for others. You can pray for peace in the world. You can ask for mercy and forgiveness.

You can also ask God for anything you desire. In fact, asking God for whatever it is you want is what many people consider a prayer to be. Jesus said: "What things soever ye desire, when ye pray, believe that ye receive them, and ye shall have them" (Mark 11:24). Obviously, the hardest part of a prayer of this sort is to believe that it's possible. God doesn't have what you desire, but is the substance of that desire. Consequently, if you have enough faith, and ask for it seriously and sincerely, you can ask God for anything.

---

5. Saint Teresa of Ávila, quoted in *Encyclopaedia Britannica*, vol. 14 (Chicago: Encyclopaedia Britannica, Inc., 15th edition, 1983), 948.

There should be no conditions attached to your prayers. If you pray to God asking for ten million dollars, and promise that if you win it you'll give half of it to charity, you are negotiating, not praying.

You must be completely honest. If you pray and tell God how happy you are that your best friend won the promotion you were after, you may be stretching the truth. You are more likely to feel annoyed and angry because you thought you were the better candidate. If this is the case, you should tell God how angry you are, and how much you had wanted the promotion. Once you have done that, you can ask for forgiveness and then move on to other matters.

There is no need to repeat your request over and over again in the same prayer. This indicates a lack of faith and a lack of trust in the power of prayer. Jesus said: "But when ye pray, use not vain repetitions, as the heathen do: for they think that they shall be heard for their much speaking. Be not ye therefore like unto them: for your Father knoweth what things ye have need of, before ye ask him" (Matthew 6:7–8).

Jesus also recommended that you pray in secret: "But thou, when thou prayest, enter into thy closet, and when thou hast shut thy door, pray to thy Father which is in secret; and thy Father which seeth in secret shall reward thee openly" (Matthew 6:6). This means that you should find a quiet spot in which to pray, and the results will manifest where you can see them.

Jesus added a vital element that is often overlooked: "And when ye stand praying, forgive, if ye have ought against any: that your Father also which is in heaven may forgive you your trespasses. But if ye do not forgive, neither will your Father which is in heaven forgive your trespasses" (Mark 11:25–26).

Jesus's final suggestion was that you finish your prayers by reciting the Lord's Prayer: "After this manner therefore pray ye: 'Our Father which art in heaven, hallowed be Thy name. Thy kingdom come, Thy will be done in earth, as it is in heaven. Give us this day our daily bread. And forgive us our debts, as we forgive our debtors. And lead us not into temptation, but deliver us from evil: for Thine is the kingdom, and the power, and the glory, for ever. Amen'" (Matthew 6:9–13).

I have met many people who can recite the Lord's Prayer but have never given a thought to what it means. The message is straightforward and direct. "Our Father in heaven" means that you are addressing God directly. "Hallowed be thy name" shows that God's name is sacred. "Thy kingdom come" shows the kingdom of heaven is waiting for all of us. "Thy will be done in earth, as it is in heaven." This shows that God's divine will look after everything in His time. "Give us this day our daily bread" simply means that you are asking for bread today. "And forgive us our debts, as we forgive our debtors" shows that you are asking for forgiveness, in the same way you forgive others. "And lead us not into temptation, but deliver us from evil" means that you are requesting to be kept well away from anything that could be evil or overly tempting. "For Thine is the kingdom, and the power and the glory, for ever" means you are acknowledging God as the source of everything. The Lord's Prayer is concise, but it covers almost everything.

Jesus believed we could all achieve anything using the power of faith, prayer, and forgiveness.

Does Prayer Work?

Every now and again, someone asks me if prayer works. I doubt that people would have continued praying throughout human history if they weren't convinced that it worked. Most people prove the effectiveness of prayer in their own lives, but some studies have been done that reveal the power of prayer.

In 1988, Dr. Randolph Byrd conducted a study at San Francisco General Hospital, using 393 patients who had been admitted with heart attacks and severe chest pain. All the patients received the best attention possible, but in addition to this, half of the patients were prayed for. To make the experiment as conclusive as possible, none of the doctors, nurses, or patients knew who was being prayed for. When the results were checked later, it was found that fewer of the prayed-for patients had died, and none of them had required the mechanical ventilator. Twelve patients in the group that were not prayed for required the ventilator.[6]

Another well-documented example concerned a seventeen-year-old girl in Uganda named Juliet. In 1989, a man with AIDS raped her. One year later, she was diagnosed as HIV-positive. Juliet had not told her parents about the incident. She lost a great deal of weight and was distraught and suicidal. In desperation, she visited a well-known healer named Pastor Simeon Kayiwa. He told her that he would pray and fast for

---

6. Larry Dossey, M.D., "Medicine, Meaning and Prayer." Article in *The Power of Meditation and Prayer* (Carlsbad, CA: Hay House, 1997), 4–5.

her, and she would have to do the same. Juliet did not believe this would work, but had no other option. During the following months, Juliet had three medical tests, all of which showed she was still HIV-positive. Pastor Kayiwa insisted she would recover. He said he would pray for her three more times, and then she would have to visit her doctor.

Late in 1991, she retuned to her doctor and the tests proved negative. Three later tests all proved negative. Her mother, unaware of what had happened, was delighted when Juliet started putting on weight. She asked her what had happened. "Jesus works," Juliet replied. Pastor Kayiwa later healed Juliet's sister, who now visits a hospital two days a week to pray for the patients. "Prayer is the best medicine I know of," a now healthy Juliet says.[7]

Why Pray?

The main reason to pray is to experience God. Some people would say that this is the only reason to pray, as prayer opens us up to the divine and enables God to work with and through us. Consequently, you do not need a specific purpose in mind when you pray.

You should pray to God on a regular basis. Many people pray when the situation is desperate, but make no attempt to communicate with God at any other time. These people would find it hard to believe that there are people who pray to God all day, every day, following Saint Paul's advice to "pray without

---

7. Rochelle Gibler, "AIDS: The Documented Cures," in *Miracles*, vol. I, No. I (1994), 10. Further information on Pastor Kayiwa is in Rochelle Gibler, "The Documented Miracles of Simeon Kayiwa," in *Miracles*, vol. I, No. 3 (1995), 25–26.

ceasing" (I Thessalonians 5:17). The nineteenth-century Russian religious classic *The Way of a Pilgrim* follows the path of an anonymous spiritual seeker who sought enlightenment by praying unceasingly.[8]

Few people are able to pray constantly, but everyone has the ability to communicate with the divine at odd moments through the day. The perfect scenario is to have a special place and time every day to quiet your mind and body and to pray. However, most people lead busy lives and have to seize spare moments as and when they can. Lying in bed before going to sleep is a good time to pray. Brief prayers can be made while you are waiting in line at the bank, post office, or supermarket. I've prayed at traffic lights while waiting for them to turn green. A local church has recently instituted prayer walks, which combine physical fitness and exercise. The idea is that members of the congregation go on a brisk walk and pray silently, instead of chatting with each other. It's an interesting concept that shows you can pray anywhere, at any time. We all have many moments during the day when we could pray, if we wanted to.

There are many benefits to this. You will experience an immediate sense of comfort, hope, and peace, as if a huge weight has been lifted off your shoulders. Your stress levels will diminish as you realize your concerns are being attended to by a higher power. You will sense your close connection with the divine. You will accept that God has your best interests at heart

---

8. Anonymous, *The Way of a Pilgrim*. Many editions available. My copy is *The Way of a Pilgrim and The Pilgrim Continues His Way*, translated by Helen Bacovcin (New York: Image Books, 1978).

and will do everything possible to help you. As a result, your relationship with God will become closer and closer, and every aspect of your life will improve.

Another interesting benefit is that praying goes well beyond our normal logical selves and opens the door to intuitive insights. This is one reason why people suddenly gain knowledge of the right course of action after praying. Prayer takes us well away from our own small, limited perspective, and enables us to receive an answer from the universal mind, which knows everything.

Choosing a Prayer Position

Many people think the only way to pray is on bended knees. However, as we have seen, people can pray in bed just as easily as they can when out walking. There is no one correct way. In fact, the Bible mentions several possibilities:

KNEELING

"Now when Daniel knew that the writing was signed, he went into his house; and his windows being opened in his chamber toward Jerusalem, he kneeled upon his knees three times a day, and prayed, and gave thanks before his God, as he did aforetime" (Daniel 6:10).

SITTING

"The went King David in, and sat before the Lord, and he said, 'Who am I, O Lord God? And what is my house, that thou hast brought me hitherto?'" (2 Samuel 7:18).

STANDING

"And Solomon stood before the altar of the Lord in the presence of all the congregation of Israel, and spread forth his hands toward heaven" (I Kings 8:22).

WALKING

"And what doth the Lord require of thee, but to do justly, and to love mercy, and to walk humbly with thy God?" (Micah 6:8).

BOWED HEAD

"And the man bowed down his head, and worshipped the Lord" (Genesis 24:26).

RAISED HANDS

"I will therefore that men pray everywhere, lifting up holy hands, without wrath and doubting" (I Timothy 2:8).

FACE DOWN

"And Moses and Aaron went from the presence of the assembly unto the door of the tabernacle of the congregation, and they fell upon their faces: and the glory of the Lord appeared unto them" (Numbers 20:6).

How to Pray

People frequently tell me they don't know how to pray. This is a common problem. Even Saint Paul wrote: "We know not what we should pray for as we ought: but the Spirit itself maketh intercession for us with groanings which cannot be uttered" (Romans 8:26).

There are no special techniques for a successful prayer. I find the best way for me is to relax my body and mind first, as doing so puts me in a meditative state that feels right for me. Most of my students found that this method worked for them, too. However, there were exceptions. One of my students prayed when she was working out on a treadmill. Another prayed while waiting at a bus stop. Several waited until they were in bed at night and prayed while waiting for sleep. One sang his prayers.

All of them felt that praying simply worked better than prayers composed of flowery, old-fashioned, or formal-sounding words. The intent behind the prayer was more important than the actual words.

Prayer is an intimate communication with the divine. As none of us know who or what "God" is, no one can tell you the correct way to pray. You are making a personal communication with the universal life force, and whatever way works best for you is the correct method.

The Experience of Prayer

People experience the act of prayer in different ways. Some people feel that they are enfolded in God's embrace while praying. Many people feel as if they are in an altered state, which, in fact, they are. Some people experience a profound sense that they are communicating with the divine and that their prayers will be answered. Virtually everyone experiences a sense of peace and a knowledge that "thy will be done" (Matthew 6:10, Luke 11:2).

When you consider all the benefits that come as a result of prayer, it's surprising that many people never pray. If you have not prayed for a long time, start by reciting a prayer or two from your childhood. You will be amazed at how powerful the simplest of children's prayers can be. If you have never prayed before, start with a simple prayer of thanks. You might say something like this: "Dear God, thank You for all the blessings in my life. Please bless and help [list here all the important people in your life]. Thank You, God. Amen."

The Centering Prayer

You might also experiment with a prayerful meditation, called a centering prayer, in which you focus on a single word or phrase, repeating it again and again in your mind. You might use "love" or "vibrant health," for instance. I prefer to close my eyes while doing this, but you can also do it with your eyes open. You will find that your thoughts will wander from time to time while you are doing this, which is perfectly normal. Once you become aware of your thoughts, acknowledge them. Then return to your mantra.

The purpose of a centering prayer is to instill the sacred word or phrase into your subconscious mind, where it will actively draw you toward the divine.

To finish the centering prayer, stop repeating the sacred word or phrase and sit quietly with your eyes closed for a minute or two. When you feel ready to return to your everyday world, open your eyes and get up.

Angels and Prayer

Many people find the thought of praying directly to God a daunting, or even presumptuous, prospect. They don't want to bother God with their problems. These people find it less intimi-dating to pray through an intermediary. This is why, throughout history, angels have been used to transport prayers to heaven. We'll look at the role angels play in prayer in the next chapter.

TWO

Angels

Angels are supernatural beings of thought who mediate between God and mankind. The main function of angels has always been to transmit messages between mankind and God. Angels also attend to, and worship, God, but their main role is that of messenger.

Today, angels are normally pictured as chubby cherubs with wings. However, they can appear in any shape or form they wish, depending on the situation. Most of the time they appear in human form, and the people they meet may not even realize they've spent time with an angel.

According to Jewish tradition, angels were created on the second day of Creation. Unlike humans, they are not constantly evolving and growing. They were born perfect and fully aware of their role in sustaining the universe according to God's wishes.

Throughout history, angels have delivered messages from God. There are numerous mentions of angels and angelic contact in the Bible. In one of the first mentions of an angel in the Bible,[9] a young, pregnant servant girl called Hagar was fleeing from Abram's wife, Sarai. The "angel of the Lord" appeared to her and told her to return home. He also told her she would give birth to a son named Ishmael (Genesis 16:7–12).

The Archangel Gabriel is God's chief messenger. She announces special events of great spiritual importance. Christians believe her most important message was telling Mary she would give birth to the Son of God. Many Christians also believe that it was Gabriel who announced the birth of Christ to the shepherds in the fields and warned Mary and Joseph to flee to Egypt when Herod's soldiers were looking for the newborn King.

Gabriel is also the most important messenger in Islam. It was Gabriel who dictated the Koran to Muhammad. Gabriel also took Muhammad on a magical nighttime tour of all seven heavens.

Angels also deliver messages from people to God. Catholics often pray to specific angels, knowing that God will hear their request. Angels are always present when people pray.

---

9. The first mention of an angel is in Genesis 3:24, immediately after Adam and Eve had been banished from the garden of Eden: "So he drove out the man; and he placed at the east of the garden of Eden Cherubims, and a flaming sword which turned every way, to keep the way of the tree of life."

Angels also have other tasks. They constantly attend to the Throne of God (Genesis 32:1; Psalms 103:21; Kings 22:19; Job 1:6). They possess a strong sense of what is right and wrong (2 Samuel 14:17–20). They rejoice at every sinner who repents (Luke 15:10). They are prepared to punish the wicked when it is necessary (Genesis 22:11; Exodus 14:19; Numbers 20:16; Psalms 34:7). They can change their form at will. The famous words in Hebrews 13:2 relate to this: "Be not forgetful to entertain strangers: for thereby some have entertained angels unawares." Like me, you've probably entertained angels and realized it afterwards, too.

The Angelic Doctor

During his lifetime, Saint Thomas Aquinas (c. 1225–1274) was known as the "angelic doctor." He described angels as "purely spiritual, intellectual and non-corporeal creatures, with 'substances.'"[10] He was a prolific writer. In the *Summa Theologiae*, he gave detailed answers to 118 questions about angels, and provided five proofs for the existence of God. In the *Summa contra Gentiles*, he provided eight proofs that angels existed. He taught that everyone has a guardian angel, and this angel stays with the person throughout life, no matter how good or bad the individual happens to be. He believed that although guardian angels do not prevent people from doing evil things, they constantly try to inspire their humans to do the right thing. Saint Thomas Aquinas believed that people need angels because

10. Thomas Aquinas, quoted in Karl Barth, *Church Dogmatics*, trans. G. W. Bromiley (Edinburgh: T and T Clark, 1960), vol. 3, 391. Originally published in German as *Kirchliche Dogmatik*.

people do not know the secrets of their own hearts. Until they ultimately meet their maker, they need to rely on the enlightenment and understanding they gain from communicating with their guardian angels.

Meister Eckhart (c. 1260–c. 1327), the German theologian and mystic, believed that angels are purely spiritual beings. He wrote: "That's all an angel is, an idea of God."

Emanuel Swedenborg (1688–1772), the Swedish theologian and scientist, thought that only the pure in heart can see angels, and that they see them through their souls.

The Language of the Angels

John Dee (1527–1608) was an alchemist, mathematician, and scholar. He used astrology to advise Queen Elizabeth I on the best possible day for her coronation, and he also made important discoveries in navigation. He gave valuable advice to mariners engaged in seeking new routes to the Far East and the New World, and helped to write the first English translation of Euclid's works. Despite his high reputation and standing, he was always considered a suspect character because of his interest in angels.

John Dee spent much of his time communicating with angels, using Edward Kelley, a gifted medium, as his scryer. In his notebooks, Dee described how the angels communicated with the pair and dictated the Enochian language, the language of the angels, to them. This language must be the most remarkable example of information received from the angelic realms. The Enochian language has its own alphabet, syntax, grammar, and numerical system. Although Edward Kelley was a dubious character, it appears impossible that he could have invented a complete language, especially in the extremely complex way it was communicated to him.

Saint Teresa of Ávila

At the same time that John Dee was communicating with angels in Mortlake, London, Saint Teresa of Ávila (1515–1582), a Spanish mystic, was seeing them in Spain. She recorded in her autobiography that her confessors were convinced her visions came from Satan.

Her most profound angelic experience occurred in 1559 and is known as "the transverberation of Saint Teresa." The word "transverberation" means "to strike through." Saint Teresa recounted the experience in her autobiography: "He was not tall but short, and very beautiful; and his face was so aflame that he appeared to be one of the highest rank of angels, who seem to be all on fire. They must be of the kind called cherubim, but they do not tell me their names."[11] This angel held a golden spear which he thrust into Saint Teresa's heart several times. When he pulled the sword out, she was in agony, but totally consumed with the love of God. After this experience, Teresa vowed to do everything she could to please God.

---

11.   Saint Teresa of Ávila, *The Life of Saint Teresa of Avila by Herself*, trans. J. M. Cohen (London: Penguin, 1987), 210.

Paradise Lost

John Milton (1608–1674) was one of the greatest poets in the English language. His epic poem *Paradise Lost* tells how Satan tempts Eve in a dream that encourages her to eat the forbidden fruit from the Tree of Knowledge. Gabriel and Ithuriel find Satan and eject him from the Garden of Eden. After Eve tells Adam about her disturbing dream, Raphael appears and encourages Adam to be obedient. He tells him about Satan and the story of the good and evil angels. Satan reappears in the guise of a serpent and again encourages Eve to eat the fruit. This time he succeeds. Adam realizes what has happened and eats the fruit too, so he can perish with her. Satan returns to hell and tells the other angels of his success. All the angels in hell temporarily turn themselves into serpents. God sends the Son of God to judge Adam and Eve. After hearing the story and their repentance, he acts on their behalf. God decides the punishment to be expulsion from the Garden of Eden, and Michael is sent down to escort Adam and Eve from the garden.

John Milton's epic poem is still being read today, but its account of the war in the heavens and the actions of the angels and Satan are fictional, and the characters appear to be more human than angelic. Many Christians detest this poem, as it shows Satan in a heroic light.[12]

---

12. Duane A. Garrett, *Angels and the New Spirituality* (Nashville: Broadman and Holman, 1995), 93.

Emanuel Swedenborg

Emanuel Swedenborg (1688–1772) was a Swedish scientist who became a mystic after a personal crisis provoked dreams and visions that convinced him he could contact the spirit world. Before this crisis, he had written books on algebra, navigation, chemistry, and astronomy. From 1743 on, with the help of the angels he conversed with every day, he started writing theological books about heaven and hell. His most famous book, *Heaven and Hell*, was published in 1758. Swedenborg's angels in heaven live lives remarkably like ours. They wear clothing and live in houses, which are grouped into villages, towns, and cities. They eat food, marry each other, listen to good music, work in useful occupations, and generally lead dull and unexciting lives.

William Blake

William Blake (1757–1827), the English poet, artist, and mystic, saw a tree full of angels on Peckham Rye, South London, when he was about eight years old. He continued to have visions for the rest of his life. He recorded one of the most momentous of these in his diary. While trying to create an angel for a book commission, he asked out loud: "Who can paint an angel?" Instantly, he heard the reply: "Michelangelo could."

"How do you know?" Blake asked the anonymous voice.

"I know, for I sat for him. I am the Archangel Gabriel."

Blake was still not entirely convinced and suggested the voice might belong to an evil spirit.

"Can an evil spirit do this?" the voice replied.

Blake became aware of a bright shape with large wings. The shape radiated with pure light. The angel grew bigger and bigger, and the roof of Blake's study opened up as Gabriel ascended up to heaven. Blake wrote in his diary that Gabriel then "moved the universe." Unfortunately, Blake did not explain how this occurred, but he did write that he was convinced he had seen Gabriel.

Guardian Angels

Whether or not you are aware of it, you have a guardian angel who was assigned to you at conception and who will remain with you until after you have experienced physical death. In fact, some people, including Rudolf Steiner (1861–1925), the founder of Anthroposophy, believe that your guardian angel stays with you through all your incarnations, and not just your present lifetime.

Your guardian angel's task is to protect, guide, and look after you throughout this lifetime. He looks after your soul as well as your physical body. Messages from your guardian angel are received as thoughts and intuitions. This is the "still small voice" that spoke to Elijah on Mount Sinai (1 Kings 19:12). As it is quiet and gentle, it can often be overlooked. You must be prepared to listen to and receive messages from your guardian angel. At the end of your life, your guardian angel will carry your soul to heaven.

The early Christian fathers believed that every person has a guardian angel. Jesus intimated that children have guardian angels when he said: "Take heed that ye despise not one of these little ones; for I say unto you that in heaven their angels do always behold the face of my Father which is in heaven" (Matthew 18:10). Hermas (c. second century CE), author of *The Shepherd of Hermas*, believed that everyone has both a guardian angel ("angel of righteousness") and a demon ("angel of iniquity"). Belief in guardian angels grew throughout the fourth century. Basil the Great (c. 330–379) wrote: "Among the angels, some are in charge of nations, others are the companions of the faithful . . . It is the teaching of Moses that every believer has an angel to guide him as a teacher and a shepherd."[13] The concept of a guardian angel is still part of Catholic belief today.

Sadly, many people are not aware of their guardian angel. Most of the time, your guardian angel will quietly watch over you, offering advice only when it's asked for. Everyone makes mistakes and blunders at times, and I am often asked why our guardian angels don't interfere and prevent these from happening. The reason is that we learn from our mistakes, and they frequently provide the lessons we need to learn in this incarnation. Guardian angels often communicate with us in the form of dreams. It is always up to us whether or not we act upon the insights we gain this way.

Occasionally, guardian angels act in a direct manner. Sir Ernest Shackleton (1874–1922), the British explorer, knew that "one more" accompanied his party as they trudged back from the South Pole. Francis Sydney Smythe (1900–1949), the British mountaineer, became aware of an invisible companion when

---

13. Basil, Adv. Eun., 3.1, cited in Jean Daniélou, *The Angels and Their Mission*, trans. David Heimann (Dublin: Four Courts Press, 1957), 68. Originally published in French as *Les anges et leur mission*.

he was attempting the final stage of his ascent of Mount Everest. "I could not feel lonely, neither could I come to any harm," he wrote afterwards.

Hierarchy of Angels

There are also many other angels that you can call upon for different purposes. Theologians seem to enjoy classifying angels into different groups or hierarchies. The most famous of these was created by Dionysius the Areopagite in the sixth century and was included in his book *The Celestial Hierarchies*. His system contains nine ranks of angels:

1. Seraphim
2. Cherubim
3. Thrones
4. Dominions
5. Virtues
6. Powers
7. Principalities
8. Archangels
9. Angels

This hierarchy is also divided into three groups, known as triads or choirs. The highest ones are closest to God's throne and are involved in work that is intended to help the entire universe. The angels in the lowest triad (principalities, archangels, and angels) help God look after the earth. This explains why archangels are the second to lowest in the list, even though archangels are on each side of God's throne.

First Triad

1. **Seraphim**. The seraphim have six red wings that glow. Two wings cover their feet, two their faces, and the other two are used for flying. They carry flaming red swords and chant, "Holy, holy, holy is the Lord of Hosts; the whole earth is full of His glory" as they circle God's throne.

2. **Cherubim**. The cherubim wear deep blue clothes and carry swords to protect the way to the Tree of Life at the east gate of Eden. The prophet Ezekiel saw four cherubim and described them as having four faces and four wings (Ezekiel 1:10–11).

3. **Thrones**. The thrones are the judiciary angels who administer divine judgment and ensure that God's truths are imparted to everyone.

Second Triad

4. **Dominions**. The dominions determine what cosmic responsibilities need to be attended to and supervise the tasks and duties of each angel.

5. **Virtues**. The virtues work out the necessary strategy to get the responsibilities underway. They provide confidence, courage, and blessings.

6. **Powers**. The powers carry out the plans. They also protect heaven from demonic attack and watch over people's souls, even guiding lost souls on their way to heaven.

Third Triad

7. **Principalities**. The principalities organize the tasks that need to be performed on earth. They have a special interest in spiritual matters and the welfare of nations.

8. **Archangels**. With the archangels, we are finally able to identify individual angels by name. The archangels carry out the tasks organized by the principalities. They are the most important of God's messengers.

9. **Angels**. The angels are the ones who are closest to us. The angels in the ninth position are the humblest angels, yet they have the enormous responsibility of interacting between God and humankind. Our guardian angels belong to this group.

All of the angels, no matter what group they belong to, look after and pay attention to every other angel. Dante Alighieri (1265–1321) explained this in his *Divine Comedy* when he wrote:

And all these orders upwards gaze with awe,

And downward each prevails upon the rest,

Whence all are drawn to God and to Him draw.

Why Are Angels Willing to Help Us?

I am sometimes asked why angels are so willing to help us. All we need do is ask for help when it is required, and God and his angels will come to our aid. All you need do is ask, have faith, and a response will come. It may not happen in exactly the shape or form you desired. Sometimes you will experience help in the form of a dream that helps to clarify the situation. On another occasion, a series of apparent coincidences will ensure the right outcome. God works in mysterious ways.

In Psalm 91:11–15, David gave a beautiful explanation of why angels are willing to help us:

"For he shall give his angels charge over thee, to keep thee in all thy ways. They shall bear thee up in *their* hands, lest thou dash thy foot against a stone. Thou shalt tread upon the lion and adder: the young lion and the dragon shalt thou trample under feet. Because he hath set his love upon me, therefore will I deliver him: I will set him on high, because he hath known my name. He shall call upon me, and I will answer him: I *will be* with him in trouble; I will deliver him, and honor him."

Can Anyone Communicate with Angels?

Yes, angels are happy to communicate with anyone. It makes no difference what religion, if any, you may belong to. You can ask for divine help anytime you need it. The only requirement is your faith in the universal life force.

How Will I Know If a Message Is from an Angel?

I am also frequently asked: "How will I know if a feeling or message comes from an angel?" This is a difficult question to answer. Sometimes you will experience a definite sense of knowing. It might be an intuition or gut feeling, or a knowledge that everything will turn out the way it should. Most of the time we don't question where our feelings come from. Every now and again, ask yourself if a certain intuition has come from an angel, and then wait for a response. Frequently, you will find it is an angelic message. I believe that most, if not all, intuitive flashes are angelic messages.

Sometimes it's impossible to answer. If the desired outcome has been achieved through an extraordinary series of coincidences, or serendipity is involved, you can assume that angels have orchestrated the result, but you will never be able to prove it. The best response is to accept the outcome with gratitude and give thanks to the angelic kingdom.

Is It Bad to Pray to Angels?

Some people consider it idolatrous to pray to angels rather than directly to God. However, no less a person than Pope Pius XI (1857–1939) prayed to his guardian angel twice every day. He told a group of visitors that whenever he had to speak to someone who he thought might not accept his ideas, he asked his guardian angel to speak to the other person's guardian angel first. The two guardian angels invariably came to an understanding that allowed the meeting to proceed without any difficulty.[14]

Way back in the fourth century, Ambrose (c. 339–397), an early church father, wrote: "We should pray to the angels who are given to us as guardians."[15]

When you pray to angels, you are not worshipping them. You are simply asking the angel to intercede on your behalf. In

---

14. Harvey Humann, *The Many Faces of Angels* (Marina del Rey, CA: DeVorss and Company, 1986), 5–6.

15. Ambrose, quoted in *A Select Library of the Nicene and Post-Nicene Fathers of the Christian Church*, ed. Philip Schaff (Edinburgh: T and T Clark, 1989), vol. 10, *De Vidius*, section 9.

actuality, you are praying *with* an angel, who will then deliver the prayer.

I consider angels to be part of the universal mind. Consequently, when I pray to an angel, I am, in a sense, praying to God. This may sound confusing. Why not pray directly to God, rather than to an underling? I do, in fact, pray directly to God, too. Whom I pray to depends entirely on the prayer.

We will discuss how to pray with angels in the next chapter.

❧ THREE

How to Contact the Angels

You can include the angels in any prayer you make. You might ask your guardian angel to deliver your prayer for you, or you might ask a specific angel who has a deep involvement with the topic of your prayer to deliver it for you. (A dictionary of angels can be found in the appendix.)

You can ask the angels to pray with you whenever you choose. However, if you have not prayed with the angels before, it is helpful to become familiar with them first. Once you have done this, communication with the angelic kingdom will be much easier.

How to Gain Angel Awareness

Set aside some time when you will not be disturbed. If you are doing this indoors, you might find it helpful to temporarily disconnect the phone. Sit down in a comfortable chair, close your eyes, and relax. I prefer sitting to lying down, as I'm inclined to fall asleep when performing this exercise on a bed.

Focus on your breathing, and take ten slow, deep breaths. Inhale, hold the breath for a few moments, and then exhale slowly. As you exhale, say silently to yourself: "Relax, relax, relax."

Once you feel totally relaxed, forget about your breathing and think about your desire to communicate with your guardian angel. Thank your guardian angel for his presence, advice, and support. Tell your guardian angel how much you'd like to make regular contact and ask if this is possible. Pause and see what response comes to you.

You may be fortunate and receive an immediate response. If this occurs, you can express your love and gratitude to your guardian angel right away. You can then ask your guardian angel for any advice or help you may need.

There is no need to feel disappointed if you fail to receive a response on the first, second, or even tenth attempt. You have lived on Earth for a number of years already without trying to make contact. Your guardian angel may simply be testing you to see how sincere and determined you are.

The communication, once it comes, may not occur in the way you expect. You may hear a voice inside your head imparting knowledge and advice. You will not confuse your guardian angel's communications with the random thoughts we experience all day, every day. The messages from your guardian angel will have a different energy from your regular thoughts. The voice will seem more vibrant, and the messages will give you knowledge and insights that you would not otherwise know.

You may experience communication in the form of dreams and wake up in the morning with the information you need. It is not always easy to determine if messages that come through dreams are actually from your guardian angel or from your subconscious mind. However, over a period of time you'll realize that dream messages from your guardian angel are of a higher quality than insights gained from your mind.

You may experience messages in the form of signs. White feathers are a common example of this. It seems strange to me now, but for many years I didn't accept the common belief that white feathers are a sign of angelic communication. For years after writing *Spirit Guides and Angel Guardians*, my first book on angels, people asked me to write another. I always replied that one book on the subject was enough. However, I gradually became aware that I wanted to write about the archangels but for some reason kept putting it off. After delaying the project for several months, I started finding white feathers everywhere. This was the sign I needed. I stopped fighting the idea and started writing a series of books on the archangels.

The signs can occur in a variety of forms. You might start finding small-denomination coins. An acquaintance of mine experiences a beautiful scent that tells her contact has been made. A lady at a talk I gave told us that she hears a strange whistling noise that acts as a sign. Be alert for anything out of the ordinary that could be a form of angelic communication.

Another extremely pleasant form of communication occurs when the problem you have discussed with an angel is suddenly resolved. In these cases, the angel will have manipulated circumstances to create a solution that is fair to everyone concerned.

Once you have made contact, you need to establish regular communication with your guardian angel. Initially, you should do this with regular relaxation sessions. However, once you are experienced and have gained confidence with this, you should experiment with communicating with your guardian angel at other times.

You can make contact at different times during the day. A brief communication at work will give you energy and make you more productive for the rest of the day. If you travel by public transport, you could put that time to good use and contact your guardian angel. You can also do this while stuck in traffic, waiting in line, or before going to sleep at night. In fact, any time you have a few minutes to yourself is a good time to make contact.

Writing to Your Guardian Angel

Writing a letter to your guardian angel is a highly effective way of making contact. The time, thought, and effort you put into writing a letter concentrates your energies. Consequently, it is not surprising that some people accidentally contact their guardian angel while in the process of writing the letter.

There is no need to write in a formal manner. You should write the letter as if writing to a close friend. Obviously, you should have a purpose in writing the letter. If you have not yet made contact with your guardian angel, you might write asking for a closer connection. If you have already made contact, you can ask your guardian angel for anything you need. This can include asking for help for other people.

In addition to this, you should tell your guardian angel what is going on in your life. Tell your angel about your family, relationships, work, plans, and dreams. You will find this beneficial in a number of ways. Writing your hopes and dreams down forces you to clarify them in your mind. This effectively turns them into goals that you can then pursue. Problems and difficulties in your life are put into their proper perspective when you record them on paper. Everyday worries don't seem nearly as bad when you write them down.

Once you have finished the letter, thank your guardian angel for looking after you. Express your love and sign your name. Seal the letter inside an envelope and write "To My Guardian Angel" on the front.

It is possible that your guardian angel made contact while you were writing the letter. This is the ideal situation, as you can stop writing and enjoy a heart-to-heart talk. It is more likely that you will not hear from your guardian angel while writing the letter. When this occurs, you need to "mail" the letter to your angel.

Sit in front of a lit candle with the envelope in your cupped hands. Think about what your guardian angel does for you and offer thanks. When you have said everything you wish to say, burn the envelope in the candle flame and watch the smoke carry your message to your guardian angel. Whisper a final "thank you" as the smoke rises; then carry on with your day, confident that your guardian angel has received your letter.

Obviously, you need to be careful when you do anything with candles. I like to place my candles on metal trays, and I always have water available, just in case of an accident. I have never needed the water, but I feel happier when I know that every precaution has been taken.

Candle Meditation

This is a wonderful method of making angelic contact. You can perform it at any time, but it is most effective in the evening with no light other than the candle flame. You can use any candle as long as it appeals to you. I love candles and have a large selection to choose from. Most of the time, I instinctively know what color candle to choose. At other times, I make a deliberate choice based on the meanings of the different colors. Here are the standard color associations:

- *Red* provides confidence, energy, and passion.
- *Orange* provides motivation and eliminates fear, doubt, and worry.
- *Yellow* stimulates the mind and helps open, honest communication.
- *Green* relieves stress, impatience, and anger. It also provides stability and contentment.
- *Blue* helps overcome nervousness and indecision.
- *Indigo* provides faith and helps you handle family problems.
- *Violet* provides inner peace and nurtures the soul.

- *Pink* helps you overcome emotional difficulties and helps you to give and receive love.
- *Gray* helps overcome mental exhaustion.
- *Silver* provides confidence and self-esteem.
- *Gold* eliminates negative feelings about success and financial improvement.

You can use a white candle for any purpose. Whenever you find it hard to decide which candle to use, choose a white one.

Place a lit candle on a table about six feet (about two meters) away from where you will be sitting. The flame of the candle should be at about the level of your third eye when you are sitting down. Take a few slow, deep breaths and gaze at the flickering flame. You will find this extremely relaxing, and your eyes may want to close. Resist this, and think of your desire to contact your guardian angel (or any other angel). Keep gazing into the flame. After a few minutes you might sense, or even catch a glimpse of, an angel. When this happens, start communicating with your angel, silently or out loud.

Walking with an Angel

My favorite way of making angelic contact is to walk with an angel. I enjoy walking and go for a walk almost every day. Frequently, I will ask an angel to walk with me. This is usually my guardian angel, but I also call on other angels from time to time. I set out on my walk in the usual way. After walking for about five minutes, I'll invite an angel to walk with me. After a minute or two, I'll become aware that an angel is walking with me. I won't see or hear this angel, but will experience a strong sense of his presence. Once I realize the angel has joined me, I'll start talking with him. I've learned from experience that it's better to do this silently rather than out loud. The angel's answers appear as thoughts in my mind. Once I have discussed everything I need, I'll thank the angel and finish the walk on my own.

Once you get used to walking with an angel, you'll find that you can do it anywhere, even in a crowded shopping mall.

Chakra Meditation

The chakras are energy centers situated in the aura. They absorb and distribute physical, mental, emotional, and spiritual energies. The seven main auras are situated between the base of the spine and the top of the head. When they are well balanced, they keep your mind, body, and spirit harmonized and in balance, creating feelings of happiness and well-being. Well-balanced chakras also enhance spiritual awareness. Every chakra has a purpose.

1. The first, or base, chakra is situated at the base of the spine. It is concerned with survival, security, and physical activities.

2. The second, or sacral, chakra is situated in the lower part of the abdomen, above the genitals. It is concerned with sexuality, sensuality, and the fluidic functions of the body.

3. The third, or solar plexus, chakra is situated about an inch above the navel. It is concerned with willpower, confidence, and happiness.

4. The fourth, or heart, chakra is situated at the same level as the heart. It is concerned with love, harmony, compassion, relationships, and emotions.

5. The fifth, or throat, chakra is situated in the area of the throat. It is concerned with self-expression and creativity.

6. The sixth, or brow, chakra is situated just above the level of the eyebrows. It is concerned with imagination, intuition, and thought.

7. The seventh, or crown, chakra is situated at the top of the head. It is concerned with higher consciousness, spirituality, and our link to the divine.

Any blockages cause problems in the person's life. A blocked second chakra, for instance, would create problems with the proper functioning of the reproductive system. Likewise, a blocked fourth chakra would create problems in expressing emotions.

Everybody experiences involuntary reactions from their chakras at different times. Have you ever felt so choked with emotion that you felt your heart would burst? Have you ever felt a constriction in your throat when you tried to express something of vital importance? These are times when the chakras, which are normally invisible and working behind the scenes, make themselves apparent.

When the chakras are perfectly aligned, your connection with the universal life force is at its strongest. This is the perfect time to communicate with your guardian angel. It is an eight-step process:

I. Sit in a straight-backed chair with your feet flat on the floor. Alternatively, sit cross-legged on the floor with your spine and head forming a vertical line. It is important that you feel comfortable and relaxed.

2. Close your eyes and focus on your base chakra at the base of your spine. Visualize it as a spinning wheel of energy, and sense the energy it produces.

3. Move your focus to your sacral chakra in your lower abdomen. Visualize it as a spinning wheel of energy. Sense the difference between the energies of your base and sacral chakras.

4. Continue moving up through the chakras. Focus on each one until you can clearly sense its energy. If you find it hard to pick up the energy from any of them, take three or four slow, deep breaths and visualize the air revitalizing and energizing the particular chakra that needs attention.

5. Once you have sensed each chakra, visualize energy from your base chakra moving up your spine, through each chakra in turn, up to the crown chakra.

6. Hold the energy there and silently ask your guardian angel to join you. When you sense your angel has arrived, let the energy flow heavenwards from your crown chakra.

7. Speak to your guardian angel for as long as you wish. When you have finished, thank your guardian angel and say goodbye.

8. Visualize your guardian angel leaving. When you feel ready, take three slow, deep breaths and open your eyes.

Circle of Joy

The Circle of Joy is a magic circle that you create around your-self. It is a special, sacred space that you can use to perform any form of spiritual work within. With practice, you will be able to mentally visualize a circle around yourself, but it is better to start by creating a physical circle several feet in diameter. In practice, I do both. Sometimes I enjoy creating a circle, while at other times I'll visualize it. I have a large circular rug that frequently acts as my circle when I'm working indoors. You can create your circle from anything you wish. Some people like to create a circle out of rope, while others prefer to place small objects, such as candles or stones, in a circle around them-selves.

When you have created your circle, place a comfortable chair in the center. Walk around the circle a few times, and then sit down on the chair and make yourself comfortable. Close your eyes and imagine a beautiful white light filling the circle with protection. You'll feel safe and secure inside your Circle of Joy. This is a quiet, secure place that you can come to whenever you wish. You can use it to relax and unwind, to think things through, or to communicate with your angels.

When you feel ready, ask your guardian angel to join you. Sit quietly and comfortably until you know she has arrived. Once you have greeted each other, you can discuss anything you wish. Depending on where your circle is, you can talk silently or out loud. When you have finished your conversation, thank your guardian angel for all she is doing for you. Sit quietly for another minute or two, and then open your eyes. Stand up, stretch, and when you feel ready, leave your circle.

Your circle is portable. You can create it wherever you happen to be. You will find it a pleasant escape from the pressures of everyday life, and an excellent place to meet your guardian angel.

Circle of Protection

This is a slightly more advanced version of the Circle of Joy, and incorporates Raphael, Michael, Gabriel, and Uriel, the four great archangels. It is an incredibly powerful and moving experience to perform this rite. Ideally, you should not experiment with it until you have mastered the Circle of Joy.

It is a good idea to have a shower or bath before performing the Circle of Protection. This symbolically purifies you. Many people also change into special loose-fitting clothes, such as robes, to further separate themselves from their everyday lives.

Use a rope or a selection of small objects to create a circle. Stand in the center of your circle and face east. Close your eyes, and imagine white light descending from the heavens. Visualize it filling you and your magic circle with divine protection. When you sense that you are completely surrounded by white light, say "thank you" out loud.

You are now ready to call on the great archangels. Open your eyes and visualize Raphael standing directly in front of you. People "see" the archangels in different ways. You might see him as a bearded, robed figure, holding a staff and a fish. This is how he is traditionally drawn. However, it is more likely that you'll sense him as energy or as a rainbow of color. It makes no difference how you experience him, just as long as you know he is there. When you first start experimenting with this, you might have to imagine he's there. Once you sense that Raphael is in front of you, extend your right arm and hand, with the first two fingers extended, directly in front of you. Starting from the bottom left-hand side, draw an imaginary pentagram (five-sided star) in the air. Once you have done this, bring your hand back a few inches, and then make a stabbing motion through the center of this pentagram.

Keep your right hand extended as you turn ninety degrees to face south. This time visualize Michael as clearly as you can. Again, you might see him as a bearded figure holding a set of scales, or he might appear as whirls of color or light. Once you sense he is there, make the sign of the pentagram again, finishing by making a stabbing motion in the center. With your arm still extended, turn another ninety degrees to face west, and visualize Gabriel. Once you have a clear picture of her, make a pentagram in the air, stab it, and then turn to face north. This time visualize Uriel. Once you have him clearly in mind, construct a final pentagram, stab it, and turn to face east again.

You are now completely surrounded by the four great archangels and can perform anything you wish inside your circle, knowing that you are completely protected. Thank the archangels for their help and protection and discuss anything you wish with them. You can also pray to God and communicate with any member of the angelic kingdom while you are in the circle.

When you are ready to close your circle and carry on with your day, face east once more and thank Raphael for his love and care. Turn to the south and thank Michael, followed by Gabriel and Uriel. Finally, face east again, say "thank you" in any way that seems appropriate, and step out of the circle.

This ceremony can be an emotional one. Allow as much time as necessary before carrying on with your day. You will find the Circle of Protection will give you unlimited energy as well as insight into what is going on in your life.

Members of the Hermetic Order of the Golden Dawn use a similar ritual starting with what they called a Qabalistic Cross. After visualizing the circle filling with white light, they help the process by reaching skyward with their right hands and symbolically pulling the white light down. They continue the movement by making a sign of the cross on their bodies by touching their forehead, navel, and each side of their chest while saying "For thine" (while touching forehead), "is the kingdom" (while touching stomach), "the power" (touching right side of chest), "and the glory" (touching left side of chest). They continue by holding both hands over their heart while saying "for ever through the ages." They finish this part of the ritual by extending their arms on each side to simulate a cross. I almost always perform the Qabalistic Cross as I find it instantly puts me into the desired spiritual state of mind. Experiment with both methods and see which one appeals most to you.

Angelic Protection

Once you have learned how to contact the angelic kingdom, you will be able to ask the angels for help whenever you find yourself in a potentially difficult situation. We're all inclined to overreact or become angry when we feel we're not being treated with fairness or respect. Asking for angelic protection ensures that you will remain calm, relaxed, and in control in situations that might previously have been stressful or potentially dangerous.

The technique is a simple one that can be performed in a matter of seconds. However, you will have to practice it until you have it mastered. Once you know exactly how to do it, you'll find your life will become easier and smoother, as you'll no longer overreact or become angry inappropriately.

When you are practicing this, you will need to think of something that is causing difficulty in your life. This exercise will enable you to handle it much more easily than before.

Sit down in a comfortable chair, close your eyes, and take a few slow, deep breaths. Allow yourself to relax. I find it helpful to silently say, "Relax, relax deeply" each time I exhale.

Once you feel completely relaxed, imagine a clear white light coming down from heaven and enveloping you in its protective light. Ask your guardian angel, or any other angel who seems appropriate for the situation, to join you and help you handle the concern.

You'll find that the presence of an angel will prevent you from doing or saying anything you might regret later. In fact, you'll be able to handle the situation in a sympathetic, understanding manner that takes in the views of everyone involved. One of my students said she felt "saint-like" the first time she used this technique.

You should practice this technique until it becomes second nature. That way, when you are suddenly confronted with a difficult situation, you'll have instant angelic aid and protection.

Obviously, you should use this technique whenever you are seriously threatened. If your physical well-being is being threatened, you should call on Archangel Michael to give you instant help and protection.

Now that you know how to contact the angels, we will start looking at specific groups of angels, starting with the angels of the four elements.

FOUR

Angels of the Four Elements

The four elements of fire, earth, air, and water are spiritual principles that have been used for thousands of years to symbolize the fundamental building blocks of the universe. Empedocles of Acragas, a follower of Pythagoras, is credited with discovering the four elements twenty-five hundred years ago.[16] The ancient Chinese system of five elements (wood, fire,

---

16. John Michael Greer, *The New Encyclopedia of the Occult* (St. Paul, MN: Llewellyn, 2003), 151.

earth, metal, and water) goes back even further and is at least four thousand years old.[17]

Everything in the universe can be classified according to earth (solids), water (liquids), and air (vapor). All three of these can be converted from one to another using fire (energy). Ice is a good example. When ice is heated it turns into water. If the heat continues, it becomes steam. Candles are popular tools in many rituals. This is partly because they represent all four elements. The solid candle symbolizes the earth element; liquid wax symbolizes water; the flame symbolizes fire; and the smoke symbolizes air.

The elements all have large lists of associations and correspondences. Plato (c. 428–347 BCE), for example, classified all living beings in this way. He placed beasts into the element of earth, fish into water, birds into air, and stars into fire. Medieval magicians and alchemists assigned gemstones, heavenly bodies, shapes, personality types, directions, seasons, tarot and playing-card suits, gods, and even angels to the different elements. These correspondences are still being used in magic today.

17.   Udo Becker, *The Continuum Encyclopedia of Symbols*, trans. Lance W. Garmer (New York: Continuum, 1994), 98. Originally published in German as *Lexikon der Symbole* (Freiburg, Germany: Verlag Herder, 1992).

Here are some of the more common correspondences:[18]

AIR

Age: Birth

Angel: Chassan

Archangel: Raphael

Astrological signs: Gemini, Libra, and Aquarius

Color: Yellow

Direction: East

Jewel: Topaz or chalcedony

Metal: Mercury

Season: Spring

Tarot suit: Swords

FIRE

Age: Youth

Angel: Aral

Archangel: Michael

Astrological signs: Aries, Leo, and Sagittarius

Color: Red

---

18. These are the most commonly accepted correspondences. However, there have always been variations. Here are two examples: *The Magical Calendar of Tycho Brahe*, dating from Renaissance times, lists an alternative arrangement of the elements. In this system, Raphael is associated with fire; Michael with air; Gabriel with water; and Uriel with earth. Raphael and Michael have changed positions. (David Allen Hulse, *The Key of It All* [St. Paul, MN: Llewellyn, 1994], xlvii.) Arthur Edward Waite, the celebrated author and occultist, changed the earlier association of air with the suit of wands, and fire with the suit of swords, in the tarot deck. He associated wands with fire and swords with air. As the Rider-Waite tarot is still the most popular Tarot deck available, many people have accepted the changes he made. (Deborah Lipp, *The Way of Four: Create Elemental Balance in Your Life* [St. Paul, MN: Llewellyn Publications, 2004], 5.)

Direction: South
Jewel: Fire opal
Metals: Iron or gold
Season: Summer
Tarot suit: Wands

WATER
Age: Middle age
Angel: Taliahad
Archangel: Gabriel
Astrological signs: Cancer, Scorpio, and Pisces
Color: Blue
Direction: West
Jewels: Aquamarine or beryl
Metal: Silver
Season: Autumn
Tarot suit: Cups

EARTH
Age: Old age
Angel: Phorlakh
Archangel: Uriel
Astrological signs: Taurus, Virgo, and Capricorn
Color: Black
Direction: North
Jewel: Quartz
Metal: Lead
Season: Winter
Tarot suit: Pentacles

There are many reasons why you might choose to pray with an elemental angel. Communicating with Phorlakh, the angel of the earth, for instance, helps you keep your feet firmly on the ground. Communicating with Chassan, angel of the air, helps you regain vital energy. At its most basic, prana or ch'i energy is air. Talking with Taliahad, angel of the water, helps to restore your emotional balance. Spending time with Aral, angel of fire, helps you regain enthusiasm and zest for life and creates a thirst for knowledge.

Here are other topics that you can discuss with the elemental angels:

FIRE

Positive: Change, energy, power, courage, strength, purification, freedom, ambition, drive, and motivation.

Negative: Possessiveness, anger, hate, lust, and egotism.

AIR

Positive: Intellect, mind, knowledge, discrimination, clarity, inspiration, happiness, and logic.

Negative: Anxiety, impulsiveness, insecurity, and fear.

WATER

Positive: Sensuality, sexuality, intuition, femininity, dreams, womb, compassion, sympathy, understanding, and the subconscious.

Negative: Jealousy, hatred, deceit, treachery, backbiting, and spite.

EARTH

Positive: Nature, survival, health, well-being, stability, responsibility, substance, growth, and practicality.

Negative: Procrastination, laziness, stubbornness, greed, and melancholy.

You can also discuss health matters with the elemental angels. The angel of earth will help with matters concerning bones, muscles, and skin. The angel of fire will help with energy, digestion, circulation, and respiration. The angel of air will help with matters concerning breathing. The angel of water will be happy to help with matters concerning blood and bodily fluids.

Basic Requirements

You can contact the elemental angels using the methods we've already discussed. However, there are also a number of ceremonies that are specifically designed to contact the elemental angels.

There are a few requirements. Firstly, you will need an altar. You might have a table or sideboard that can be dedicated solely to communicating with the angels. Most people do not have that luxury and instead use part of a kitchen table, or a card table, coffee table, or any other flat surface that is available. I enjoy performing these rituals outdoors when the weather is suitable. I may use a tree trunk, a rug, or a cloth placed on the ground, or even a flat area of land, as an impromptu altar.

You will also need to collect some tools to symbolize the four elements. As mentioned earlier, a candle can be used to symbolize all four elements, and it will work well if nothing else is available. However, you will find it well worth the time and effort required to collect attractive objects to represent each of the elements.

Earth

Traditionally, this was a circular disc with a pentagram inscribed on the front and a hexagram on the back. The pentagram symbolized the microcosm (mankind) and the hexagram the macrocosm (the universe). A disc of this sort is called a pentacle. However, it is not essential. A round wooden platter will perform the same function, and have the advantage that it can also hold fruit or cake.

Some people use a drum to represent the earth element. An earthenware container of rock salt can also be used.

Air

A dagger has traditionally been used to represent the element of air. Any sharp knife can be utilized for this purpose. A flute, or any other wind instrument, can also be used. If you prefer, you might choose incense and candles as well, or instead.

Fire

Wands have always symbolized power, command, and special powers. You can buy specially made wands at many New Age shops, but an attractive branch between one foot and two feet long will serve just as well. If possible, find a branch that has already fallen from a tree. Cut a branch from a tree only if nothing else is available.

Water

You will need an attractive object that can hold water. Traditionally, this was a chalice, but a wine glass can be used for the same purpose. If you are performing an impromptu ritual, any container that will hold water will do.

Consecration

Once you have the necessary tools, you will need to consecrate them before using them to contact the angels. It is best to do this in the form of a simple ritual in front of your altar.

In addition to the tools, you will need a small amount of salt, a candle, and water. Place these on your altar. Have a bath and change into fresh, loose-fitting clothes.

Stand in front of your altar and light the candle. Cast a magic circle around yourself. You might create a Circle of Protection as described in chapter 3, or, alternatively, visualize yourself surrounded by a Circle of Protection.

Face east and ask Chassan, angel of air, for his blessing. Pause until you sense that the blessing has been given. Turn to the south and ask Aral, angel of fire, for his blessing. Once you have received it, turn to the west and ask Taliahad, angel of water, for his blessing. Turn to the north and call on Phorlakh, again asking for a blessing.

You are now safe inside your circle, surrounded by the angels who have given you their blessing on this consecration ceremony. It is time to consecrate the objects you have selected.

Face your altar and pick up the object that you will be using to symbolize air. We will assume it is a dagger. Hold the dagger high in the air for a few moments; then bring it down and pass it through the smoke produced by the candle. As you do this, say out loud: "I hereby purify and consecrate you with the strength and power provided by the element of air." Visualize beneficial air surrounding and purifying your dagger as you pass it through the flame.

Hold the dagger high up into the air again, and then pass it through the flame of the candle, this time saying: "I hereby purify and consecrate you with the strength and power provided by the element of fire." As you say this, visualize a burning fire removing all the negativity from the dagger.

Hold the dagger up high again before placing it gently on the altar. Dip your fingers into the container of water and sprinkle the dagger with a few drops of water while saying: "I hereby purify and consecrate you with the strength and power provided by the element of water." Visualize purifying water washing away any negativity that might still be attached to the dagger.

Pick up the dagger and hold it as high as you can. Replace it on your altar and sprinkle it with a few grains of salt. Visualize the dagger buried in earth and being drained of any negativity as you say: "I hereby purify and consecrate you with the strength and power provided by the element of earth."

Repeat this procedure with the other three objects. When you are finished, place the four newly consecrated objects on your altar in a row and thank them for becoming your sacred objects.

Finish the ritual by thanking each of the angels in turn. Start with Chassan in the east. Face his direction, thank him for his protection, and say goodbye. I generally smile and wave my hand as I say goodbye. After you have done this, face north and say goodbye and thank you to Phorlakh. Continue with Taliahad and Aral. You will notice that you have ended the routine by saying goodbye to the angels in a counterclockwise direction. Working in a counterclockwise direction is known as widdershins.

Spend a minute of two in quiet contemplation and then leave the circle. You might want to wrap your consecrated objects in silk when you are not using them. These are now special, sacred objects, and you should not let anyone else handle them.

Communicating with the Elemental Angels

You can create a basic ritual for contacting the elemental angels using the structure we used for consecrating the sacred objects.

I. Place a white candle and your sacred objects on your altar. You can use as many candles as you wish. You can also place anything else on your altar that you consider spiritual or that relates to your reason for conducting the ritual. If, for instance, you are conducting a ritual to ask the angels to help heal a sick friend, you might decide to place a photograph of that person on the altar.

2. Have a bath and change into fresh clothes. You might prefer to wear a robe that is used solely for ritual work. Alternatively, depending on the temperature and circumstances, you might like to work skyclad (naked).

3. Create a magic circle to work within. This can be a physical circle, or you might prefer to visualize one.

4. Step inside the circle and light the candle(s).

5. Close your eyes and visualize the circle being filled with white light.

6. Perform the Qabalistic Cross (see chapter 3.)

7. Pick up the dagger in your right hand and face east. Call on Chassan, angel of air. You can speak to him silently or out loud. Point the dagger slightly upwards in front of you. Wait until you sense his presence. Replace the dagger on your altar.

8. Pick up the wand and face south. Call on Aral, angel of fire. Hold your wand high in front of you and wait for a response. Place the wand back on the altar.

9. Pick up the chalice and face west. Call on Taliahad. Hold the chalice in both hands and raise it to shoulder height. Once you have received a response, replace the chalice on the altar.

10. Pick up the pentacle and face north. Call on Phorlakh. If you are using a traditional pentacle, hold it high in your right hand. If you are using a wooden dish or bowl, hold it at chest height with both hands. Place the pentacle back on the altar after you have received a response.

11. Spend a minute or two enjoying the sensations of safety and security inside the circle. Feel the energies of the four angels that surround you.

12. When the time feels right, talk to the angels about your concerns and make your request. Face whichever angel relates best to whatever it is you are discussing. However, make sure that you include all of the angels in your conversation. Pause every now and again to see if you receive a direct response from them. Talk in a

normal, conversational manner. In my experience, the angels prefer a normal conversation to grand-sounding, archaic words such as "Oh mighty angels, praise be to you for aiding mankind from the time of Adam. I, unworthy miscreant that I am, beseech you to offer succor," and so forth.

13. Take as long as you wish. The angels want to help you and will not become impatient if you take your time. Sometimes the conversation might last a few minutes, while at other times it might take an hour. It makes no difference just as long as you mention everything you intended to.

14. Thank the angels jointly and separately for their help. Ask them to send your request to God. This ritual is, in effect, a prayer. Say goodbye to each angel individually, starting with Chassan in the east and working widdershins so that you finish with Aral in the south.

15. Put out the candle(s). Stay inside the circle until you feel ready to return to your everyday world.

16. Step outside the circle.

Leave the implements on your altar until later. You might pack them up after you've changed back into your normal clothes. You will find that your consecrated objects will feel more and more spiritual every time you use them. Keep them in a safe place.

The above is a basic format for a ritual involving the elemental angels. You might prefer to write your request in the form of a letter and then send it to heaven by burning it. You might like to say some favorite prayers or sing a psalm. You might like to beat a drum and dance inside the circle. What you do is entirely up to you. It is your ritual and as long as you perform it sincerely, it makes no difference what you do.

Once the ritual is over and everything has been packed away, you can carry on with your life, confident that the angels will be working on your concern for you. Repeat the ritual as often as you wish until you receive the desired result.

You can perform a similar ritual invoking the archangels if your purpose involves healing the planet in any way.

How to Eliminate Negativity

The angels of the four elements will be happy to help you eliminate any negativity in your life, including negative thoughts and feelings you might be hanging on to, as well as any negativity aimed at you by others. Negative emotions—such as anger, jealousy, and resentment—can be eliminated with this ritual, too. Start by finding a dark-colored stone or pebble that you can comfortably clasp in one hand. You will also need a source of running water, such as a river, stream, or the sea. It is best to perform the ritual outdoors, close to the water supply, but if necessary you can perform the ritual at home and take the stone to the water afterwards.

Here is the basic ritual:

1. Prepare for the ritual in the usual way by taking a bath and changing into fresh, loose-fitting clothes.

2. Create a magic circle around your altar.

3. Hold the stone in your right hand as you step inside the circle.

4. Light a white candle and place it in the center of your altar. Place the stone on your altar a few inches in front of the candle.

5. Close your eyes and visualize the circle being filled with white light.

6. Perform the Qabalistic Cross (see chapter 3.)

7. Greet each of the angels in turn, starting with Chassan in the east and continuing in a clockwise direction with Aral, Taliahad, and Phorlakh.

8. Thank the angels for coming to your help and tell them about the negativity that is going on in your life. Ask them for their help in eliminating it. Pause until you sense their assent.

9. Pick up the stone and face east. Hold the stone against your stomach and allow any negativity from this region to flow into the stone. Some people find this highly emotional. Allow your emotions free rein. Feel free to cry, shout, stamp your feet, or do anything else that helps you release all the negativity from your solar plexus. If you find it hard to let the negativity go from your solar plexus, then give it a shape and a color. Visualize the shape becoming smaller and smaller until it is a tiny speck. In your mind, flick it out of your body and into the stone. Some people feel no emotion at all when performing this ritual. If this occurs, place the stone back on the

altar and rhythmically tap your stomach with the fingers of both hands for sixty seconds, and then pick up the stone again.

10. Hold the stone to your forehead and allow any negativity from this part of your body to flow into the stone. Negative thoughts are sometimes reluctant to leave. If necessary, give them a shape and color, reduce them in size, and flick them into the stone. Tap your forehead with the fingers of each hand if necessary.

11. Place the stone against your heart and allow any negative emotions to leave your body and enter the stone.

12. Hold the stone in your cupped right hand and rest this hand in your left palm. Slowly raise both hands to shoulder height and ask Chassan to seal all the negativity into the stone. When you sense this has been done, ask him to bless and purify you.

13. Repeat step 12 with the other angels, again moving in a clockwise direction. Finish by facing east again.

14. The stone is now full of your released negativity. This negativity is sealed inside and cannot be released until the stone is cleansed with running water.

15. If you are performing this ritual beside a source of flowing water, thank the stone for helping you in the ritual, and then throw it into the water with as much force as possible. Ensure that it is completely submerged in the water. If you are performing the ritual somewhere else, place the stone back in front of the candle.

16. Thank the angels individually for helping you to eliminate the negativity. Thank them also for all their kindness and attention.

17. Say goodbye, starting with Chassan in the east, and working widdershins through Phorlakh, Taliahad, and Aral.

18. Extinguish the candle and spend as long as you desire inside the circle. When you feel ready, leave the circle and carry on with your day.

19. This ritual can be emotionally draining, and you might be surprised with the effect it has on you. Eat and drink as soon as possible after the ritual to restore your energy. Nuts, raisins, and fruit juice are ideal.

20. All the negativity is sealed inside the stone. However, you should toss it into flowing water as soon as possible after the ritual. If it is not possible to do this until the next day, place the stone outside overnight.

The long-term results of this ritual can be life-changing. However, most people find it hard to let go of all their negativity at one time. Consequently, you should perform this ritual frequently until you are certain that all the negativity has been released. We all pick up negativity as we go through life. For this reason, you should perform this ritual every few months to ensure you remain as positive as possible.

The Power of Salt

Salt has been used in religion and magic for thousands of years, probably because of its incorruptibility, purity, and value. For primitive people, salt was rare and essential for preserving food during the long, cold winters. Salt became a symbol of vitality and good health. The word "salt" comes from the Roman goddess of health, Salus.

Salt also became a symbol of spirituality, and Jesus referred to his disciples as the "salt of the earth" (Matthew 5:13). This means they were supposedly incorruptible, and possessed the strength and power represented by salt. The incorruptibility of salt is referred to in the Bible when "the covenant of salt" referred to a covenant that God could not break (2 Chronicles 13:5). The Jewish people considered the communal eating of bread and salt to indicate a friendship that could never be broken. In fact, the ancient Greeks, Jews, and Muslims all considered salt to be a symbol of hospitality and friendship. Someone who is referred to as the "salt of the earth" is considered an upstanding, honest person.

Salt also provides protection and is still used in holy water today to ward off evil. At one time, salt was placed in coffins to provide protection from the devil. A small amount of salt in a cradle was believed to protect an unchristened child. In British folklore, it was believed that if the parents of a baby brought salt to the baptism, the child would be certain to enter heaven. Even today, some people toss salt over their left shoulder to avert bad luck or evil influences.

Alchemists also used salt, sulfur, and quicksilver (mercury) in their rituals to symbolize the philosophical elements of life.

Salt belongs to the earth element and can be used in a variety of ways to provide protection and increase prosperity. In the past, salt was frequently sprinkled around doors and windows to avert potential demons and other evil energies.

Sea salt is usually used in rituals. However, ordinary table salt can be used if sea salt is not available. The salt you use in ritual work should be kept separate from your household salt.

Salt for Protection

Salt can be used to protect any space. You might want to protect part of a room, such as the area you perform your rituals in, or you might want to protect your entire home.

To protect a room:

1. Mix a small quantity of salt in pure water. You might buy a bottle of spring water or, alternatively, purify ordinary tap water by placing it in a clear glass container and exposing it to several hours of both sunlight and moonlight.

2. Sprinkle a few drops of the salt water in each corner of the room, and follow this by doing the same in the center of every door and window.

3. Create a magic circle in the center of the room. Hold the container of salt water at chest height and ask the angels of each quarter to bless it.

4. Close the circle, but leave the container of water in the center of the room for twenty-four hours.

The procedure is exactly the same for protecting the entire house. Sprinkle water in each corner of the house, and also in the center of any doors and windows that lead outdoors. Create a magic circle in the most important room of the house, and leave the container of salt water in this room for twenty-four hours. The most important room of the house is usually the living room, or any other room that the family members congregate in. However, in your case, it might well be the kitchen, a bedroom, a porch, or any other room that you consider central to your concept of home.

Salt and Prosperity

Soldiers in ancient Rome were sometimes paid in salt. This is where the expression "worth his salt" comes from. The word "salary" comes from the Latin *salarium*, which means "salt allowance."

You can perform rituals for anything you wish. However, there has to be a specific need. You are unlikely to achieve your goal if you conduct a ritual for "tons of money." You need to specify the exact amount required and the purpose it will be used for. You also need faith, patience, and the ability to seize any opportunities that present themselves for achieving the goal. A magic spell is unlikely to do the task entirely on its own. Sooner or later, you will be presented an opportunity as a result of the spell, and it might take a considerable amount of work and effort to make it happen.

If you have a specific financial goal in mind, here is a simple ritual to help you achieve it. You will need some new coins. As they are symbolic, the exact denomination of them is unimportant. In Chinese folklore, the number eight means money in the near future. Consequently, I always use at least eight coins. You also need four yellow or gold candles and a few tablespoons of salt.

1. Start by placing the items you need (candles, coins, and salt) on your altar. Ensure that the room is warm enough for the ritual.

2. Enjoy a leisurely bath. If possible, use bath salts. They help the ritual by symbolically surrounding you with salt before the ritual begins. You may also choose to burn candles in the bathroom. If possible, use yellow or gold candles to symbolize abundance. These candles should be burned in the bathroom only. You will need additional candles for the ritual. Spend as long as you wish in the bath, and think about your desire. Dry yourself with a clean, thick bath towel. Change into clean, loose-fitting clothes.

3. Before starting the ritual proper, use a spoon to form a mound of salt in the center of your altar. Three or four tablespoons are sufficient to symbolize abundance. Surround the salt with a circle of coins. Create this circle in a clockwise direction. Ideally, the coins should overlap each other to symbolize abundance. Place the candles outside the circle of coins in the four cardinal positions (east, south, west, and north).

4. Create a magic circle around your altar. Take a pinch of salt from the heap on your altar and sprinkle it at the cardinal points on your circle. Welcome the angels of the elements.

5. Light the four candles.

6. Sit or stand in front of your altar and gaze at the salt in the center. Visualize it being transformed into the sum of money you require for your purpose. See it as clearly as you can in your mind. I like to visualize it as a mountain of gold coins that entirely covers the altar and spills onto the floor, ultimately carpeting my entire magic circle.

7. Hold the image of this in your mind for as long as you can. When it fades, give thanks for the abundance you are seeking.

8. Snuff out the candles, thank the angels of the elements, and close the circle.

9. Leave the room for at least thirty minutes. When you return, gather up the coins in a counterclockwise direction and place them in an open container. Scoop up the salt and place it in a container. Place both of these containers in a position where they will be exposed to moonlight.

10. Repeat this ritual once a week until the first signs of your desire appear. You may find some of the money has arrived, or you may feel a sense that you are heading toward your goal. As soon as you feel this, buy a friend a surprise gift with the coins.

11. Wait for a clear evening with a visible, waxing (growing) moon. Ask Phorlakh, angel of earth, to take a leisurely stroll around your neighborhood with you. Enjoy a pleasant conversation with him, and sprinkle small amounts of salt as you go. Keep walking until all the

salt has gone. This symbolically gifts abundance to everyone in your locality. You need to give a small amount of salt to everyone, without exception. It is especially beneficial to gift abundance to people you do not care for. Continue walking for as long as you wish. Thank Phorlakh for helping you achieve the abundance you are seeking. When you feel ready, return home and enjoy a relaxing bath or shower before going to bed.

12. Do whatever work is required to reach your goal.

Keeping a Journal

We have already covered writing letters to angels. Another effective way of maintaining angelic contact is to keep a journal. The wonderful advantage a journal has over letter writing is that it becomes a permanent record of your spiritual growth and development. A journal also becomes a friend and confidant. You can record things in a journal that you would never share with anyone else. Once you start keeping a journal, you'll sometimes wonder who's doing the writing. This is because when you look back over the pages you have already written, you will discover insights and answers that you have no memory of writing.

In your journal you can write to a single angel or to as many angels as you wish. The more you write in your journal, the closer your connection with the angelic kingdom will become.

Your journal does not need to be anything special. My first journal was a school exercise book, and I changed to a more attractive-looking cloth-bound book only when I discovered how useful the practice was and decided to continue journaling. One man I know has a small notebook that he writes in at odd moments during the day. This is perfect for him, as he would not be able to carry a large book around with him without attracting comment.

Needless to say, your angel journal is private and you need to be careful with whom you share it. In fact, I haven't shown my journal to anyone.

A journal is a useful place to write to the angels of the elements. You might write to the angel of air in springtime, for instance, and the angel of earth in the winter. Obviously, you can write to any of the angels at any time, but it sometimes feels right to contact them at their special time of the year.

Another useful practice is to contact the angel for each month and each day of the week (see the Dictionary of Angels in this book). If you have nothing specific to write about, you can simply thank the specific angel of the day for helping and protecting you.

You do not have to wait for the specific day, either. If, for example, you have an important meeting on Tuesday, you could write a message to that particular angel (Camael in this example) a few days ahead, asking for help and guidance to ensure the meeting goes well.

There's no need to be shy or self-conscious when writing to an angel. Express exactly what you're feeling. If you're feeling grumpy or sad, let your feelings out in your journal. Once you have released your feelings and have got them out of your system, you can start writing to an angel.

Do not force yourself to write if you have nothing to say. Simply write down your thanks to the angel of the day and put your journal away. At other times the words will flow freely and you might write for an hour or more. These are the occasions when you'll feel that someone else is directing the pen.

Nowadays, many people write their journals on a computer. I prefer to write my journal by hand, but you should use whatever method works best for you. I use a black ballpoint pen, but an acquaintance of mine uses at least a dozen different colors and writes with fiber-tip pens. A good friend of mine writes using a mind-mapping technique. That doesn't work for me, even though I sometimes use mind mapping when outlining my books.

If you are not used to writing, you might find it hard to start an angel journal. If this is the case, start slowly, with just a sentence or two every day. I find it helpful to write in my journal at about the same time every day. If you start an angel journal, you will start looking forward to writing in it, and your sentences will turn into paragraphs and ultimately pages.

You may have noticed the astrological signs associated with the different elements. We will look at the astrological signs and their specific angels in the next chapter.

FIVE

Your Astrological Angels

Angels have had a long association with the stars and planets. Some five thousand years ago, Assyrian, Babylonian, and Persian artists created figures of griffins, strange-looking creatures with the body of a lion, the head of an eagle, and the tail of a serpent or scorpion. They frequently had wings. The lion and eagle are two animals with a close connection to the sun. Consequently, griffins were considered benevolent beings and were used as protective guardians.

Not coincidentally, griffins contained the astrological symbols of Taurus, Leo, Scorpio, and Aquarius. This is because these signs marked the solstices and equinoxes of early Mesopotamian astrology. The bull symbolized Taurus, the spring equinox, and the east. The lion represented Leo, the summer solstice, and the south. The eagle depicted Scorpio, the autumn equinox, and the west. The water carrier symbolized Aquarius, the winter solstice, and the north.

The Jews adopted the griffins and made them cherubim, arguably the earliest angels. Consequently, the association between angels, astrology, and the four cardinal directions goes back well into our prehistory.[19]

As both angels and the astrological signs belong to the celestial realms, it is not surprising that a tradition of angels that look after and govern the twelve signs of the zodiac began. There is some disagreement about which angels are associated with which sign, but the most commonly mentioned angels are the ones listed by Johannes Trithemius (1462–1516) in *The Book of Secret Things*:

Aries: Malahidael or Machidiel
Taurus: Asmodel
Gemini: Ambriel
Cancer: Muriel

---

19. The griffin remained a symbolic animal for thousands of years. The ancient Greeks considered the griffin to be the guardian of the sun. It was sacred to Apollo. The griffin is often pictured guarding the Tree of Life. The Jews were so enamored of the griffin that they adopted it and made griffins their first angels. In the Book of Exodus, cherubim were posted in the east of Eden after the expulsion of Adam and Eve to make sure that no one entered. In early Christian times the griffin signified the human and divine nature of Christ. Griffins were popular figures in medieval Christian art and came to symbolize the two opposites of Christ and the Antichrist.

Leo: Verchiel

Virgo: Hamaliel

Libra: Uriel or Zuriel

Scorpio: Barbiel

Sagittarius: Advachiel or Adnachiel

Capricorn: Hanael

Aquarius: Cambiel or Gabriel

Pisces: Barchiel

Unfortunately, the number of angels increased so enormously in early theological literature that the rabbis became alarmed and started considering them a threat. The writings were banned, and most of the angels disappeared.[20] This was unfortunate, and it is the reason we know so little about these angels today.

The archangels were also associated with each sign of the zodiac. Originally, seven archangels looked after the seven known planets, the seven days of the week, and the seven heavens. They also looked after each sign of the zodiac.[21] These archangels are:

Sunday: Michael—Sun—Leo

Monday: Gabriel—Moon—Cancer

Tuesday: Camael—Mars—Aries and Scorpio

Wednesday: Raphael—Mercury—Gemini and Virgo

Thursday: Sachiel—Jupiter—Sagittarius and Pisces

---

20. James R. Lewis and Evelyn Dorothy Oliver, *Angels A to Z* (Canton, MI: Visible Ink Press, 1995), 423.

21. Different authorities have ascribed different angels to the days of the week. In *The Magus* (1801), Francis Barrett listed the angels as: Sunday—Raphael, Monday—Gabriel, Tuesday—Camael, Wednesday—Michael, Thursday—Zadkiel, Friday—Haniel, and Saturday—Zaphiel (pp. 126–127).

Friday: Anael—Venus—Taurus and Libra

Saturday: Cassiel—Saturn—Capricorn and Aquarius

The discovery of Uranus, Neptune, and Pluto meant three additional archangels were added to the original seven. These are Uriel, Asariel, and Azrael. Here is the revised list of planetary archangels, which most authorities consider to be the definitive list:

Aries: Camael—Mars

Taurus: Anael—Venus

Gemini: Raphael—Mercury

Cancer: Gabriel—Moon

Leo: Michael—Sun

Virgo: Raphael—Mercury

Libra: Anael—Venus

Scorpio: Azrael—Pluto

Sagittarius: Zadkiel—Jupiter

Capricorn: Cassiel—Saturn

Aquarius: Uriel—Uranus

Pisces: Asariel—Neptune

As you can see, both Anael (Taurus and Libra) and Raphael (Gemini and Virgo) appear twice.

Monthly Angels

In addition to the angels and archangels for each sign of the zodiac, there are also angels for each month of the year:

January: Gabriel or Cambiel

February: Barchiel

March: Machidiel or Malahidael

April: Asmodel
May: Ambriel
June: Muriel
July: Verchiel
August: Hamaliel
September: Uriel or Zuriel
October: Barbiel
November: Adnachiel or Advachiel
December: Anael

It is not always easy to decide when to call on an astrological or monthly angel. In practice, I call on the angel or archangel that looks after my sign for matters relating to my personal future. When making requests for someone else, I will use either the angel of the month or the angel or archangel who looks after the person's zodiac sign. Naturally, I use the angel of the month when I don't know the person's horoscope sign. For requests that do not relate to a single individual, I use the monthly angel, or whichever angel I feel would be most intimately involved in the matter.

Planetary Hours

We have already covered monthly, weekly, and daily angels. You probably won't be surprised to discover there are also angels for each hour of the day. You should use these only for requests that have specific times attached to them. If, for instance, you have a dental appointment at eleven o'clock in the morning on a certain day, you might call on the angel that looks after that particular time for help and protection. You should definitely

call on this angel if you are signing important papers or em-
barking on a potentially risky undertaking.

The planets are listed 1 to 12 for daytime hours, and 1 to
12 for nighttime hours. The planetary hours do not follow our
regular hours. The daytime hours run from sunrise to sunset,
and the nighttime hours are the opposite, running from sunset
to sunrise. Consequently, the daytime hours are much shorter
in winter than they are in summer. My daily newspaper lists
sunrise and sunset times every day. You can obtain this information from the Internet if your local paper does not provide
this information.[22] You need to divide the daytime or nighttime
hours by twelve to determine how long each planetary hour is
for the time of year you happen to be in.

SUNDAY—DAYTIME HOURS

1. Michael

2. Anael

3. Raphael

4. Gabriel

5. Cassiel

6. Sachiel

7. Samael

8. Michael

9. Anael

---

22. Sunrise and sunset times for major cities can be found on http://www.
sunrisesunset.com. That site also offers a shareware program called Sunrise
Sunset Calculator, which works out the daily sunrise and sunset times for
any reasonably sized locality around the world.

10. Raphael

11. Gabriel

12. Cassiel

SUNDAY—NIGHTTIME HOURS

1. Sachiel

2. Samael

3. Michael

4. Anael

5. Raphael

6. Gabriel

7. Cassiel

8. Sachiel

9. Samael

10. Michael

11. Anael

12. Raphael

MONDAY—DAYTIME HOURS

1. Gabriel

2. Cassiel

3. Sachiel

4. Samael

5. Michael

6. Anael

7. Raphael

8. Gabriel

9. Cassiel

10. Sachiel

11. Samael

12. Michael

MONDAY—NIGHTTIME HOURS

1. Anael

2. Raphael

3. Gabriel

4. Cassiel

5. Sachiel

6. Samael

7. Michael

8. Anael

9. Raphael

10. Gabriel

11. Cassiel

12. Sachiel

TUESDAY—DAYTIME HOURS

1. Samael

2. Michael

3. Anael

4. Raphael

5. Gabriel

6. Cassiel

7. Sachiel

8. Samael

9. Michael

10. Anael

11. Raphael

12. Gabriel

TUESDAY—NIGHTTIME HOURS

1. Cassiel

2. Sachiel

3. Samael

4. Michael

5. Anael

6. Raphael

7. Gabriel

8. Cassiel

9. Sachiel

10. Samael

11. Michael

12. Anael

WEDNESDAY—DAYTIME HOURS

1. Raphael

2. Gabriel

3. Cassiel

4. Sachiel

5. Samael

6. Michael

7. Anael

8. Raphael

9. Gabriel

10. Cassiel

11. Sachiel

12. Samael

WEDNESDAY—NIGHTTIME HOURS

1. Michael

2. Anael

3. Raphael

4. Gabriel

5. Cassiel

6. Sachiel

7. Samael

8. Michael

9. Anael

10. Raphael

11. Gabriel

12. Cassiel

THURSDAY—DAYTIME HOURS

1. Sachiel

2. Samael

3. Michael

4. Anael

5. Raphael

6. Gabriel

7. Cassiel

8. Sachiel

9. Samael

10. Michael

11. Anael

12. Raphael

THURSDAY—NIGHTTIME HOURS

1. Gabriel

2. Cassiel

3. Sachiel

4. Samael

5. Michael

6. Anael

7. Raphael

8. Gabriel

9. Cassiel

10. Sachiel

11. Samael

12. Michael

FRIDAY—DAYTIME HOURS

1. Anael

2. Raphael

3. Gabriel

4. Cassiel

5. Sachiel

6. Samael

7. Michael

8. Anael

9. Raphael

10. Gabriel

11. Cassiel

12. Sachiel

FRIDAY—NIGHTTIME HOURS

1. Samael

2. Michael

3. Anael

4. Raphael

5. Gabriel

6. Cassiel

7. Sachiel

8. Samael

9. Michael

10. Anael

11. Raphael

12. Gabriel

SATURDAY—DAYTIME HOURS

1. Cassiel

2. Sachiel

3. Samael

4. Michael

5. Anael

6. Raphael

7. Gabriel

8. Cassiel

9. Sachiel

10. Samael

11. Michael

12. Anael

SATURDAY—NIGHTTIME HOURS

1. Raphael

2. Gabriel

3. Cassiel

4. Sachiel

5. Samael

6. Michael

7. Anael

8. Raphael

9. Gabriel

10. Cassiel

11. Sachiel

12. Samael

How to Contact Your Astrological Angels

Obviously, you must have a purpose for contacting your astrological angels. There's no point in conducting a ritual simply to say hello. You could conduct a ritual to thank them for looking after you, but it is more usual to have a specific aim in mind before calling on them.

You will need four candles: one each of yellow, green, blue, and red. These will be used to mark out the magic circle and to indicate the cardinal directions. You will also need an offering to the angel(s) you call on. A slice of freshly baked cake and a glass of wine or fruit juice are ideal. Place all of these in the center of your circle before starting.

Before commencing the ritual, decide on the specific angel you wish to talk with and the best time of day to conduct the ritual. You can conduct a ritual at any time, but it is best to perform it when the moon is waxing (growing), rather than waning. The best times of day for you are the hours that relate to your astrological angel.

It is not always easy to decide on the correct angel. If you are a Libran, for instance, you might choose Anael from the list on page 74, and perform the ritual at the fifth daytime hour on a Saturday, as that time also relates to Anael. However, in this example, you might consider calling on Barbiel if your birthday is in the first few weeks of October. If you decide on Barbiel, you can still use the planetary hours associated with Anael. If your concern can be resolved within the month, you might choose the angel of the month. Choose your astrological angel for matters that cannot be resolved as quickly.

Here's another example. Let's assume your birthday is on March third, which makes you a Piscean. You could choose Asariel, the angel that looks after your sign (from the list on page 74). Alternatively, you might choose Machidiel or Malahidael, as they look after the month of March. You might choose to perform the ritual on Thursday, ruled by Sachiel, as he also looks after Pisceans. If it is not possible to perform the ritual on a Thursday, you could perform it any of the hours dedicated to Sachiel. If your concern is not of major importance, and you feel confident it will be resolved in the next few weeks, you might decide on Machidiel and perform the ritual at the second nighttime hour on a Tuesday.

Here is the basic format of a typical ritual to contact the astrological angels:

1. Start in the usual way by having a bath or a shower and changing into clean, comfortable, loose-fitting clothes.

2. Visualize your magic circle. Place the yellow candle in the east, the red one in the south, the blue one in the west, and the green one in the north.

3. Walk around the circle again, lighting the candles. Start with the yellow candle in the east and move around the circle in a clockwise direction, lighting the candles in order.

4. Invoke the four archangels to provide protection.

5. Stand in the center of your circle. Pick up the slice of cake and hold it at chest height in your cupped hands. Face east and say out loud: "I offer you, [name of angel], this cake as a token of my love and respect." Repeat this on the other cardinal points, offering the cake each time to the same angel. Face east again and slowly eat the cake. As you do so, visualize that your request has already been granted and that the desired future is already present.

6. After eating the cake, repeat step 5, using the glass of wine (or fruit juice). Place the wine glass on the ground, or on your altar, after you have drunk its contents.

7. You are now ready to summon the angel. Face east, close your eyes, and say his name seven times out loud. Picture the angel you are invoking in your mind. It makes no difference what image comes to you. Some people clearly picture an angel with large wings, while others sense colors, smells, sounds, and even shapes.

8. When you sense your angel is with you, thank him for coming to your aid, tell him your request in as much detail as possible, and then wait silently for a response. You may hear spoken words, thoughts might appear in your mind, or you might feel that everything will work out the way it should. No matter what response you receive, thank the angel sincerely.

9. At this point, you can ask further questions or discuss other matters with the angel. You are likely to sense the angel leaving your presence as he returns to the celes-

tial realms. Call out a final "thank you" and close the circle by putting out the candles, starting in the east and working widdershins (counterclockwise).

10. Rest for a few minutes before carrying on with your day. Even though you ate and drank during the ritual, it's a good idea to eat or drink something afterwards to restore your energy. You should also write down any insights you gained from the ritual as soon as possible after it is over.

Crystal Ritual

This is a simple and direct method to maintain regular contact with the angel who looks after your zodiac sign. You will need to find a gemstone or crystal that relates to the color of your sign. As there are at least three lists of color correspondences for zodiacal gems, you might prefer to find a gemstone that appeals to you, and use it, no matter what color it happens to be.

Here is a traditional list of zodiacal colors:

Aries: Yellow
Taurus: Indigo
Gemini: Green
Cancer: Orange
Leo: Red
Virgo: Green
Libra: Indigo
Scorpio: Yellow
Sagittarius: Blue
Capricorn: Violet

Aquarius: Indigo

Pisces: Blue

Here is another popular listing:

Aries: Red

Taurus: Green

Gemini: Yellow

Cancer: Silver

Leo: Gold

Virgo: Brown

Libra: Blue

Scorpio: Deep red

Sagittarius: Purple

Capricorn: Black

Aquarius: Blue

Pisces: Violet

In the late nineteenth century, the founders of the Hermetic Order of the Golden Dawn came up with their own list of zodiacal colors:

Aries: Scarlet

Taurus: Red-orange

Gemini: Orange

Cancer: Amber

Leo: Yellow, greenish

Virgo: Green, yellowish

Libra: Emerald green

Scorpio: Green-blue

Sagittarius: Blue

Capricorn: Indigo

Aquarius: Violet

Pisces: Crimson

If you fail to find a color that you like from the above lists, either use clear quartz or choose a crystal or gemstone that appeals to you.

Once you have your crystal or gemstone, you will need to consecrate it for its designated purpose of helping you make instant contact with your astrological angel. Again, you will need to perform a ritual to do so.

Place an altar or small table in the center of the area that will contain your magic circle. Place the crystal, a container of water, and a small container of salt on the altar.

Have a bath or shower before starting the ritual, and change into fresh, loose-fitting, white clothing. If you do not have any white clothes, either work skyclad or wear the palest clothes you have.

1. Mark out the magic circle—either in your mind or with physical objects such as candles—to mark the four cardinal directions.

2. Step inside the circle, light the candle on your altar, and invoke the four archangels, starting with Raphael in the east and following with Michael in the south, Gabriel in the west, and Uriel in the north.

3. Pick up the crystal that you are consecrating and hold it at chest height in the palm of your right hand, which is resting on the palm of your left hand. Face east and talk to Raphael, telling him that you wish to consecrate this crystal so that you can use it to contact your

astrological angel. The actual words you use are not important. You might say something like this: "Archangel Raphael, thank you for being with me today. I am always grateful to you for your help and protection. I ask you to bless this crystal so that I may use it to contact [name of angel], my astrological angel. Thank you." Pause until you receive a response and then turn to the south and speak to Michael.

4. After you have spoken to all four archangels and received their blessing, hold the crystal to your chest for a few moments and then place it on your altar. Talk to the crystal. "I have the blessing of the four mighty archangels to consecrate you so you may serve as my contact to [name of angel]." Pick up the crystal in your right hand. "I now consecrate you with the element of fire." Pass the crystal through the flame of the candle. "I now consecrate you with the element of air." Pass the crystal through the smoke produced by the candle. Place the crystal on the altar. "I now consecrate you with the element of water." Dip your fingers into the container of water and sprinkle some water onto the crystal. "I now consecrate you with the element of earth." Pick up some grains of salt and sprinkle them onto the crystal.

5. Pick up the crystal and again hold it in the palm of your right hand, which is resting on your left palm. Speak to the crystal. "Thank you for agreeing to help me. I will look after you to the best of my ability." Display the crystal to each of the archangels.

6. While still holding the crystal, face east and talk to your astrological angel. Notice the immediate connection you have when you are holding the crystal. Thank your astrological angel for helping you.

7. Place the crystal on your altar in front of the candle. Snuff out the candle and close the circle.

Your crystal is now ready for use. Carry it with you whenever possible. Whenever you feel the need to contact your astrological angel, hold or touch the crystal and you'll immediately be able to communicate with your angel.

Birthday Letter

This is a special letter that you can write to your astrological angel once a year on your birthday. You need to bathe and change clothes before writing it. Ideally, this letter should thank your angel for looking after you during the previous year, and also give thanks for his love, protection, and care in the year ahead. You may also—as it's your birthday—make a special request for the year ahead. You need to think carefully about this request, as you are allowed just one. The request can be for you personally or for anyone you care to name.

Once the letter has been written, seal it in an envelope and address it to your angel. Place it under your pillow for two weeks. Seeing the letter every night as you go to bed helps impress your request on your mind. It may produce dreams that relate to your desire.

If you wake up with a clear recollection of the dream, write it down as quickly as possible to ensure that it doesn't disappear as you progress with your day. If you wake up with partial recall of the dream, lie still without moving for a couple of minutes and think about the parts you do recall. Frequently, this will enable you to gain a complete memory of the dream. If you wake up knowing you've been dreaming but cannot remember it, again lie still without moving for a couple of minutes and let your thoughts go wherever they wish. Sometimes they'll take you back to your dream. There is no need to worry if you fail to remember anything. If you are meant to have the information, you will dream the dream again, and again, until you do remember it. (See chapter 8 for more information on dreaming with angels.)

After two weeks, you need to "mail" the letter. Mailing the letter is a serious business and you should make a small ceremony or ritual of it. If you belong to a fire sign (Aries, Leo, Sagittarius), you should light a white candle, think about your request, and then burn the letter, which sends it to your angel.

If you belong to an earth sign (Taurus, Virgo, Capricorn), you could either bury the letter in the ground or sprinkle it with salt (representing the earth element), and then burn it.

If you belong to an air sign (Gemini, Libra, Aquarius), you might turn the letter into a dart and release it from a high place, such as the top of a hill or tall building. Alternatively, you might prefer to pass the letter through the smoke of a candle several times before burning it.

If you belong to a water sign (Cancer, Scorpio, Pisces), you might want to make a small origami-type boat out of the letter and release it into a stream or river. Alternatively, you might prefer to sprinkle the letter with water before burning it.

With some of these methods, there is the possibility that other people might read your letter. To avoid this, you might consider writing the letter in invisible ink. Alternatively, you might use one of the many magical alphabets that have been devised over the years to ensure secrets remained concealed.

It would be hard to think of anything more important than healing. The angels play an important role in healing of all sorts. We can ask for their help in healing plants, animals, people, and even our planet. We will look at healing in the next chapter.

SIX

Healing with the Angels

We are all healers. Everyone has the power to send healing to others. Sometimes this can be as simple as a smile or a gentle touch. Years ago, I read of a man who was planning to commit suicide and happened to pass someone while walking to the bridge he planned to leap from. The stranger smiled at him, and that was enough to save his life. I'm inclined to think the stranger may well have been an angel.

Healing covers much more than curing an illness. Emotional, mental, and spiritual healing are just as important and should play a part in any healing work you do.

Raphael is the angel most often associated with healing, but every angel is willing to help you heal yourself or others. All you have to do is ask. It is usually best to discuss the matter with your guardian angel first, although you can communicate directly with any other angel if you wish.

If you are healing yourself, you will probably ask your guardian angel for help. You can do the same for animals and plants. However, it is more complicated when it comes to healing other people.

Some people have a vested interest in being ill. It may bring them attention, for instance. They might be happier lying in bed than venturing out into what they see as a dangerous and highly stressful world. Consequently, most of the time you should not send healing to someone else without his or her permission.

There will be times when you cannot obtain permission. If the person is unconscious or cannot be contacted for some reason, you can ask the angels to send healing. In this case, you can ask the angels to send whatever healing the person desires.

Many psychic and spiritual healers are helped in their work by angels, and often sense the angels' presence when they are involved in healing others. Their patients are sometimes aware of an extra pair of hands, or strong feelings of love and compassion, while the healer is working on them.

Some people are natural healers, but it is a skill that anyone who is interested can develop. Where and how far you take it is entirely up to you. Some people have a natural affinity for plants. They make wonderful gardeners because everything they look after thrives. Other people are attracted to animals. Nowadays, many people work as animal communicators, and they can use this skill to help heal the minds, bodies, and souls of the animals they work on. One pet psychic I know has a special affinity with dogs and works exclusively with them.

The Findhorn Spiritual Community

The story of Findhorn is a classic account of how a group of people were able to work with the angels to create a world-famous garden.

In 1962, Dorothy Maclean and her good friends Peter and Eileen Caddy moved to the east coast of Scotland with the intention of developing a center under spiritual guidance. Dorothy Maclean worked on their garden and soon found she was communicating with the angels, or devas, of the various plants. She began with a garden pea, and discovered that each species possesses a soul. She called this a deva, or angel.

Immediately after making this discovery, she became aware of a presence that oversaw the entire area. She called this a landscape angel. As she became more and more in tune with the angelic kingdom, she was introduced to an angel of serenity and an angel of sound. Ultimately, she met the angel of Findhorn. With the help of these angels, the trio's garden thrived and people flocked to the area to see the forty-two-pound cabbages, eight-foot delphiniums, and other plants.

Maclean wrote about her experiences in several books, including *To Hear the Angels Sing* and *The Findhorn Garden*.[23] These

---

23. Dorothy Maclean, *To Hear the Angels Sing* (Hudson, NY: Lindisfarne Press, 1994).

books have inspired many people to work with the angels in their gardens.

Raphael, Archangel of Healing

The name Raphael means "God heals." There are many stories about his healing abilities. He is believed to have healed Abraham after his circumcision. He also cured Jacob's dislocated hip, after he had spent the night fighting.[24] You can call on Raphael when you are suffering from any kind of pain. As well as physical healing, Raphael will also help with mental, emotional, and spiritual healing. You can call on him to heal the relationship between two people, for instance. You can also call on him to heal the relationship between two countries.

Raphael is the best-known angel of healing largely because of the beautiful story of Tobias and Raphael that is recorded in the *Book of Tobit*, one of the Apocryphal texts. (The Apocrypha is included in the Roman Catholic Bible, but is not part of the Protestant Bible.) This story tells how God sent Raphael to heal two people.

The first of these was Tobit, a good Jewish man who had been blind for eight years. As he was unable to make a living, his family had fallen on hard times, and Tobit sent a prayer to God asking for death. At the same moment that Tobit's prayer arrived in heaven, another arrived from a young woman named Sarah. Sarah was possessed by a demon that had killed all seven of her husbands on their wedding nights. Not surprisingly, she also found life not worth living.

---

24. Louis Ginzberg, *The Legends of the Jews, Volume 1* (Philadelphia: The Jewish Publication Society of America, 1954), 385.

Tobit began tidying up his affairs and asked Tobias, his son, to go to Medina to collect a debt. As it was too dangerous to go on his own, Tobias found a guide to accompany him. The man he chose was Raphael, but Tobias did not know that.

On the first night of the journey, Tobias and his guide camped beside a river, where a large fish tried to swallow Tobias's foot. Tobias caught this huge fish, and the guide told him to preserve the heart, liver, and gallbladder, as they could be used to make a good medicine.

As they got closer to their destination, the guide told Tobias about Sarah and suggested he marry her. Rather nervously, Tobias agreed. On the wedding night, Tobias burned the heart and liver of the fish on a fire in the bridal chamber. This exorcised the demon, who fled to "the uppermost parts of Egypt." Sarah's father was delighted and gave Tobias half of his fortune. The family returned home, and the guide told Tobias to rub the fish's gallbladder on his father's eyes. This restored his eyesight.

Tobit and Tobias were so grateful they offered half their fortune to the guide. He told them: "I am one of the seven angels who stand ready and enter before the glory of God . . . when I was with you I was not acting on my own will, but by the will of God." After this, having healed both Tobit and Sarah, Raphael returned to heaven.

Not surprisingly, the *Book of Tobit* established Raphael in his role of archangel of healing. The book also dealt with the problem of reconciling misfortune and evil with divine justice. Ultimately, both Tobit's and Sarah's faith were rewarded. This charming story also tells us that we are not alone, and that a healing angel always accompanies us. All we need to do is recognize that fact.

This story was a favorite of early Christian authors, and Renaissance artists enjoyed depicting Raphael and Tobias, usually with a fish.

Michael, Archangel of Strength and Protection

Archangel Michael also has a strong interest in healing. He is credited with creating a healing spring at Chairotopa near Colossae. This pool proved highly popular, as it was believed that anyone who bathed in the waters while invoking the Blessed Trinity and Michael would be cured. Michael also caused another healing spring to gush from a rock at Colossae. Some of the local people tried to destroy this rock, but Michael split it with a burst of lightning, which both sanctified the water and caused the stream to flow in a new direction.[25]

Michael also appeared to Emperor Constantine at Sosthenion, fifty miles south of Constantinople. As a result of this, sick people began sleeping in the church there, hoping to see Michael.

Michael is also credited with eliminating the plague that had decimated Rome. Saint Gregory, later to become pope, led the populace on a three-day procession through the streets of Rome. Eventually, they reached the Tomb of Hadrian. Gregory saw a vision of Michael standing on top of the monument, casually sheathing a bloodstained sword. Gregory realized the

---

25. Rosemary Ellen Guiley, *Encyclopedia of Angels* (New York: Facts on File, 1996), 128.

plague was over and erected a church on the site, which he dedicated to Michael.

Michael can be called upon to provide both strength and protection for people who are ill.

Sariel

The name Sariel means "the command of God." He is believed to be an archangel and is mentioned with Michael, Gabriel, and Raphael in the Dead Sea Scrolls. In the *First Book of Enoch*, he is listed as one of the seven archangels, too. In the Kabbalah, Sariel is considered one of the seven angels who rule the planet Earth. In the Talmud, Sariel is acknowledged as the angel who instructed Moses. Sariel also taught the principles of hygiene to Rabbi Ishmael and is considered, like Raphael, one of the main angels of healing.

Because of his interest in cleanliness and hygiene, Sariel is the angel to call upon for help in healing infections and other illnesses caused by lack of cleanliness or good hygiene.

Healing with Your Guardian Angel

You should contact your guardian angel for any illness that isn't life-threatening. One of my neighbors has a highly stressful job and suffers from frequent tension headaches. I suggested that she ask her guardian angel for help. She still gets headaches, though not as often as before. Whenever she gets a headache, she visits the restroom at work and spends a couple of minutes communing with her guardian angel. That is sufficient to eliminate the headache, and she is able to continue her work feeling relaxed and revitalized.

You can contact your guardian angel directly to ask for healing. Alternatively, you might include the request for healing during one of your regular communications with your special angel. Most of the time, your guardian angel will not heal you instantly. However, miracles can happen. Usually, your guardian angel will help you understand what is causing your illness, so that you can work on any underlying issues yourself.

Here is a possible outline if you'd like to create a specific healing ritual:

1. Sit down quietly in a comfortable chair. Close your eyes and relax.

2. When you feel totally relaxed, visualize the most peaceful scene you can imagine. My peaceful scenes vary, but usually include a grassy meadow, a gently flowing stream, and a pine forest. Enjoy relaxing in this peaceful scene for a minute or two and then ask your guardian angel to join you. Pause until you are certain your angel has arrived. It can be helpful to visualize your guardian angel joining you in your peaceful scene. Smile and greet him when he arrives.

3. Thank your guardian angel for looking after your best interests. Tell him about your health problem in as much detail as possible. Obviously, this may not always be easy. It is not hard to talk about a headache or a twisted ankle, but it might be complicated to discuss a ruptured appendix or diverticulitis. There is no need to dwell on the technical aspects of your illness. Your

guardian angel will know what to do to assist the healing process.

4. Ask your guardian angel for help. Visualize him laying his hands on the afflicted part of your body and feel the healing energy flowing through every cell of your being.

5. Thank your guardian angel for making you whole again. Discuss anything else you wish with your guardian angel. Once the conversation is over, thank your guardian angel again and say goodbye.

6. "Watch" him leave. Spend another minute or two in your peaceful place before taking a few slow deep breaths and opening your eyes.

7. Think about the experience for a few minutes before getting up. Write down any suggestions your guardian angel may have made during the ritual.

8. When you feel ready, carry on with your day.

You can also ask your guardian angel to communicate with the guardian angels of other people who can help you in the healing process. Before visiting a doctor, dentist, or chiropractor, for instance, you could ask your guardian angel to speak with their guardian angel to ensure you get the best possible help.

How Your Guardian Angel Can Help You Heal Others

Your guardian angel is happy to help you heal other people, too. In your sessions with your guardian angel, you can ask him to contact the other person's guardian angel and pass on your desire that the person be made whole again.

Pope Pius XI (1857–1939) prayed to his guardian angel every morning and evening. When he knew he had a potentially difficult meeting with someone, he would ask his guardian angel to contact the guardian angel of the other person beforehand. Once the two guardian angels had resolved any possible difficulties, the meeting would take place harmoniously. Not surprisingly, Pope Pius was famous for his diplomatic skills. His biggest diplomatic achievement occurred in 1929, when he ended the dispute over papal sovereignty and created Vatican City as a papal state.

The Queen of the Angels

Mary, mother of Jesus, is especially venerated by the Catholic Church, whose adherents believe she can comfort and heal people who ask for help. There have been numerous accounts of her visitations as Queen of the Angels to help people in need. Arguably, the most famous of these occurred outside Lourdes, in southwestern France, in 1858. Between February 11 and July 16, a fourteen-year-old girl named Bernadette Soubirous saw the Virgin Mary fifteen times at a grotto beside a stream near the town. Twenty thousand people came to the final visitation. The Catholic Church declared the visitations authentic in 1862, enabling the cult of Our Lady of Lourdes to proceed. More than three million pilgrims visit the site every year.

Angels have accompanied the Virgin Mary on at least four appearances: Guadalupe in 1531, Paris in 1830, Knock, Ireland in 1879, and Fatima in 1917.

You do not need to be a Catholic to call upon Mary, Queen of Angels. The best way to contact the Queen of Angels is with a simple prayer. I prefer to pray to her inside my magic circle, but this is not necessary. You can speak to her in prayer any time you wish.

Angels of Healing

One of my early mentors was Geoffrey Hodson (1886–1983), a gifted psychic, eminent author, and lifelong Theosophist. Geoffrey began studying angels in 1921, and his most remarkable angelic experience occurred three years later when he was sitting on a hillside in Gloucestershire. While he was meditating, the sky suddenly filled with light and his consciousness was taken over by the incredible radiant light. He became aware of a heavenly being who harmonized its mind with Geoffrey's, allowing him a glimpse of the wisdom of the universe. This being was an angel called Bethelda.

Bethelda explained the purposes, interests, activities, and organization of the Heavenly Host. He also told Geoffrey that angels are always ready to help people, as they want to foster a closer relationship with humans. All people need do is listen closely and observe.

Geoffrey Hodson lectured frequently at the local branch of the Theosophical Society I belonged to, and I learned a great deal from him. Geoffrey believed that angels, each of whom has a special task to perform, guide the whole cosmos. He learned from Bethelda that the angelic host could be placed into seven categories or groups.[26] These are not hierarchies, as each group is as important as any of the others. Here is Bethelda's list:

---

26. Geoffrey Hodson, *The Brotherhood of Angels and Men* (London: The Theosophical Publishing House, 1927).

1. Angels of Power. These angels are dedicated to helping humans develop spiritually.

2. Angels of Healing. These angels help people avoid illness and maintain good health. They also help people regain their health when they become ill.

3. Guardian Angels of the Home. These angels guard and protect every home.

4. Builder Angels. These angels inspire us to aspire to achieve all that we can in the areas of mind, body, and spirit.

5. Angels of Nature. These angels are the elemental spirits, sometimes called devas, that live in fire, earth, air, and water.

6. Angels of Music. These angels sing God's praises and inspire people to sing and worship God.

7. Angels of Beauty and Art. These angels provide inspiration to everyone involved in creative pursuits. They also enable everyone to appreciate beauty in all its forms.

The Angels of Healing can be called upon at any time when healing is required. Raphael is head of these angels, who work unceasingly with people who are unwell. These angels heal, provide a gentle healing touch, and provide company and consolation for the bereaved. Bethelda told Geoffrey Hodson that the healing angels struggle to help mankind, as so many people have closed minds and hearts, and this dissipates and diffuses the healing energies.

Angels of Comfort and Consolation

Several nurses have told me of their experiences dealing with patients who are dying. They are often aware of unseen presences that visit the patients, providing help, guidance, and support. Many people who have survived near-death experiences have commented on the help and compassion they have received from beings on the other side. Knowledge of this has helped many people realize that death is not the end.

The best thing you can do to help and support a friend or relative who is dying is to be generous with your time. Sit with them, reminisce, say prayers, perform errands, and talk openly and honestly about any subject they wish to discuss. One elderly lady I knew particularly enjoyed having her favorite poems read to her.

In your sessions with your guardian angel, you can ask for your love to be sent to the other person's guardian angel. Once the person has died, contact Archangel Gabriel, either directly or through your guardian angel, and ask her to help your friend or relative as he or she enters the next world.

Death is considered the final taboo. Not surprisingly, throughout history many stories have been told about the Angel of Death. One of my favorites is a Jewish tale from the fourteenth century.

An elderly man named Reuben had led an exemplary life, but became angry one day and rebuked a man who sat at his usual place in the synagogue. God saw this, and asked the Angel of Death to take away Reuben's son as punishment for his bad behavior in the synagogue. The son was about to get married, and Reuben pleaded with the Angel of Death to allow his son to get married and discover the joys of married life before taking him away. The Angel of Death was moved by Reuben's pleas and agreed.

God saw all of this and rebuked the Angel of Death for his disobedience. The Angel of Death was hurt by God's harsh words and decided to take the son after all. The prophet Elijah heard of these plans and told the son that an old man dressed in rags would arrive at the wedding. He would be the Angel of Death.

The wedding took place and the Angel of Death appeared. Reuben offered to take his son's place. However, when the Angel of Death drew his sword to cut off his head, Reuben ran away. Reuben's wife also offered herself, only to flee also. Finally, the bride offered to take her new husband's place. When she failed to run away like the others, the Angel of Death shed a tear. God decided to be merciful and told the Angel of Death to leave. God then granted both the bride and groom seventy more years of life.

Reuben's son was extremely fortunate. Few people are fortunate enough to escape the Angel of Death. This is demonstrated in a famous Jewish story from the fifth century.

King Solomon had many other talents in addition to wisdom. He was also able to understand the language of birds. One morning he heard the birds talking about how the Angel of Death was due to take two of King Solomon's closest friends and advisors. When he told them of their impending fate, they pleaded with him to help. He suggested that they flee to a magical city called Luz, because the Angel of Death was not allowed to enter it. The inhabitants of Luz will never die as long as they stay within the city walls. As the city is a magical place, its exact location was secret. Fortunately, King Solomon knew where it was and gave his two friends instructions on how to get there. His friends rode there as quickly as they could, but they were too late. Standing immediately outside the gates, waiting for them, was the Angel of Death.

Every culture has stories along these lines, showing that none of us can escape death. In the past, the Angel of Death created fear in the minds of people, as they didn't know if the angel would take them to heaven or hell. For many people, this is no longer a concern, but few of us are in a hurry to meet him.

Angels of Abundance

Whenever I talk about the angels of abundance, people immediately think in terms of money and material possessions. However, abundance means much more than that. It means a plentiful supply of all the good things in life: a fulfilling relationship, a worthwhile career, stimulating vacations, enjoyable hobbies, good friendships, excellent health, a strong faith, and sufficient money to satisfy your needs.

Many people find it hard to believe that they can enjoy abundance in every area of their lives. These people lack faith. We live in an abundant world. All you need do is look at how fruitful nature is to real-ize this.

Sadly, many people attract lack rather than abundance. They do this by constantly thinking negative thoughts. Usually it's not their fault, as poverty consciousness begins in child-hood. If your family regularly expressed thoughts along the lines of "Money doesn't grow on trees" when you were growing up, you may well have a poverty consciousness.

Fortunately, the angels of abundance are willing to help you change long-standing patterns of behavior that are affect-ing your ability to attract and enjoy all the good things of life.

Jessie Belle Rittenhouse (1869–1948), the American folk poet, wrote a famous poem called *The Wage*:

> *I bargained with Life for a penny,*
> *And Life would pay no more,*
> *However I begged at evening*
> *When I counted my scanty store;*
> *For Life is a just employer,*
> *He gives you what you ask,*
> *But once you have set the wages,*
> *Why, you must bear the task.*
> *I worked for a menial's hire,*
> *Only to learn, dismayed,*
> *That any wage I had asked of Life,*
> *Life would have paid.*[27]

---

27. Jessie B. Rittenhouse, *The Door of Dreams* (Boston: Houghton Mifflin, 1918), 25.

Do not settle for a penny when you know you are worth much, much more.

Laughter

G. K. Chesterton wrote: "Angels can fly because they take themselves lightly." Whenever you experience joy and laughter, you can be sure that angels are nearby. It does you good to be frivolous every now and again. Anything that makes you laugh is good for your soul.

Whenever you make someone else laugh, you are being blessed by angels. See if you can make at least one person laugh every day. Apart from the increased popularity you'll enjoy, you'll be constantly surrounded by joyful, happy angels.

Happiness

More than thirty years ago, my friend Lao T'zu told me: "If you want to be happy, be happy." It was wonderful, deceptively simple advice that I have tried to follow ever since. When you feel happy, you're living a life of abundance. A happy pauper enjoys a fuller, more abundant life than an unhappy multimillionaire.

Everybody has ups and downs in life. The trick is to maintain a healthy attitude no matter what is occurring. Strive to be happy when life seems gloomy and sad. Think happy thoughts and express them to others. Try to make other people happy, too. Your positive attitude can help lift other people out of their misery.

Even more importantly, whatever you express comes back to you multiplied. If you express happiness, you will receive an abundance of happiness in return. If you think in terms of prosperity, the same law applies. You will receive prosperity back. Talk health rather than sickness. People who constantly talk about their bad health experience more bad health. People who talk in terms of good health experience more good health. Talk about opportunity rather than restriction. Talk about kindness, love, virtue, and progress. If you constantly think in terms of leading a life full of abundance, the law of attraction will ensure that you'll ultimately possess it.

How to Contact the Angels of Abundance

The angels of abundance are waiting to hear from you, as they want to help you achieve your goals. All you need for this ritual are some white candles, a Bible, and faith. The number of candles is not important, but as this is a ritual for abundance, you should use more than one. I normally use eight; in feng shui, eight means prosperity in the near future.

Here is an example of a ritual involving the angels of abundance:

1. Prepare yourself in the usual way by bathing and changing into clean, loose-fitting clothes.

2. Form your circle and invoke Raphael, Michael, Gabriel, and Uriel.

3. Light the candles on your altar.

4. Recite Psalm 91, the Psalm of Serenity: "He that dwelleth in the secret place of the most High shall abide under the shadow of the Almighty. I will say of the Lord, He is my refuge and my fortress: my God; in him will I trust. Surely he shall deliver thee from the snare of

the fowler, and from the noisome pestilence. He shall cover thee with his feathers, and under his wings shalt thou trust: his truth shall by thy shield and buckler. Thou shalt not be afraid for the terror by night; nor for the arrow that flieth by day. Nor for the pestilence that walketh in darkness; nor for the destruction that wasteth at noonday. A thousand shall fall at thy side, and ten thousand at thy right hand; but it shall not come nigh thee. Only with thine eyes shalt thou behold and see the reward of the wicked. Because thou hast made the Lord, which is my refuge, even the most High, thy habitation; There shall no evil befall thee, neither shall any plague come nigh thy dwelling. For he shall give his angels charge over thee, to keep thee in all thy ways. They shall bear thee up in their hands, lest thou dash thy foot against a stone. Thou shalt tread upon the lion and adder; the young lion and the dragon shalt thou trample under feet. Because he hath set his love upon me, therefore will I deliver him: I will set him on high, because he hath known my name. He shall call upon me, and I will answer him: I will be with him in trouble; I will deliver him, and honor him. With long life will I satisfy him, and shew him my salvation."

5. Face east, close your eyes, and ask the angels of abundance to come to your aid. Spend as long as necessary in quiet contemplation until you sense their presence. Speak to them openly and honestly about your life, and tell them exactly what you want. Explain why you need

it, and whom this blessing will benefit. Tell the angels what you are prepared to do to help make your dream a reality.

6. When you have finished speaking, pause and wait to see if you receive an immediate response. You may hear words, but you are more likely to receive an answer as a thought or a feeling that all will be well. Once you have received an acknowledgment, thank the angels of abundance and say goodbye.

7. Open your eyes and read out loud the Twenty-third Psalm, the Psalm of Faith: "The Lord is my shepherd; I shall not want. He maketh me to lie down in green pastures: he leadeth me beside the still waters. He restoreth my soul: he leadeth me in the paths of righteousness for his name's sake. Yea, though I walk through the valley of the shadow of death, I will fear no evil: for thou art with me; thy rod and thy staff they comfort me. Thou preparest a table before me in the presence of mine enemies: thou anountest my head with oil; my cup runneth over. Surely goodness and mercy shall follow me all the days of my life: and I will dwell in the house of the Lord for ever."

8. Thank the archangels and close the circle.

9. Spend a few minutes in quiet contemplation before carrying on with your day. You should have a feeling of quiet confidence that your desires will be met.

You may wonder why two biblical Psalms are used in this ritual. The Psalms are full of esoteric teachings concerning the power of faith. Psalms 23 and 91 are two of the most important Psalms in this regard, and will help you achieve abundance in your life.

Evening Ritual

This is a quick ritual that you can perform in bed at night. It can be performed at any time of the day but is most effective just before you go to sleep, as your subconscious mind will work on it while you are asleep.

1. Go to bed in your usual manner. When you turn out the light, lie on your back, close your eyes, and say a simple prayer of thanks to God for the day you have just had.

2. Invite Raphael, Michael, Gabriel, and Uriel to join you. I visualize Raphael on my right, Gabriel on my left, Michael below my feet, and Uriel above my head.

3. Thank the archangels for all the help they give to you and to all of humanity. With your eyes still closed, imagine that you are looking straight up into the heavens. In your mind's eye, you might be able to see the stars and planets. Silently ask the angels of abundance to come to you. You may "see" them coming down from heaven and circling just above you.

4. Talk to the angels of abundance for as long as you wish. Listen carefully to their replies. Thank them for their help and watch them ascend into the heavens.

5. Thank the archangels for their divine protection.

6. Say another prayer to God, thanking Him for all the present and future blessings in your life. When you have finished the prayer, roll into the position you normally assume before drifting off to sleep.

7. Go to sleep.

This is a pleasant ritual that you can perform every evening if you wish. The angels will work on your behalf while you are sleeping, and you may find yourself thinking thoughts concerning abundance and plenty when you wake up in the morning.

Angels frequently communicate with us in the form of dreams. We are most receptive to angelic communication when we're relaxed and asleep. This is why we often wake up in the morning with answers to problems that seemed insolvable when going to bed. We'll look at this pleasant form of communication in the next chapter.

Dream Angels

People have always been fascinated with their dreams. The Chester Beatty Papyrus records Egyptian dream interpretations dating back almost four thousand years.[28] One thousand years later, Homer, the Greek poet, recorded in *The Iliad* how a messenger from the god Zeus visited Agamemnon in a dream. *Oneirocritica*, by Artemidorus, dates from the second century CE and is the first known book of dream interpretations.

---

28. *Encyclopaedia Britannica, Macropaedia*, volume 5 (Chicago: Encyclopaedia Britannica, Inc., 15th edition, 1974), 1011.

However, dreams were used for divination and prophecy for thousands of years before then. The people of ancient Babylonia, Egypt, Greece, Rome, and the Middle East all believed that divine will was conveyed in the form of dreams, and a variety of procedures were developed to try to interpret the messages that came through.

The Bible contains numerous references to dreams. Jacob's dream of a ladder between earth and heaven, with angels climbing up and down it (Genesis 28:12–15), was a favorite topic of Renaissance artists.

Joseph excelled at interpreting dreams. The most famous example of this was when he deciphered the pharaoh's dream about seven fat cows and seven lean cows (Genesis 41:1–7). In the Gospel according to Matthew, Joseph received two important messages from angels while dreaming. In the first, he was told: "Joseph, thou son of David, fear not to take unto thee Mary thy wife: for that which is conceived in her is of the Holy Ghost" (Matthew 1:20). Later, after the birth of Jesus: "The angel of the Lord appeareth to Joseph in a dream, saying, 'Arise, and take the young child and his mother, and flee into Egypt, and be thou there until I bring thee word: for Herod will seek the young child to destroy him'" (Matthew 2:13). After King Herod died, Joseph received another message: "Behold, an angel of the Lord appeareth in a dream to Joseph in Egypt, saying, 'Arise, and take the young child and his mother, and go into the land of Israel: for they are dead which sought the young child's life'" (Matthew 2:19–20).

Saint Patrick (c. 385–c. 461), the patron saint of Ireland, experienced a life-changing dream message from an angel. When he was sixteen, Patrick was captured by pirates and sold to an Antrim chief in Ireland. He escaped six years later, after receiving a dream message from God. Patrick took this dream as a sign that he should leave Ireland. After doing so, he had another dream, in which an angel told him to return to Ireland as a missionary. After fifteen years of study and work in France, Patrick returned to Ireland and is credited with introducing Christianity to the Irish.

In the first five hundred years of Christianity, many people paid careful attention to their dreams in the hope of discovering God's will. A number of early Christian leaders—including Iraneaus, Clement of Alexandria, Origen, Tertullian, Athanasius, Saint Augustine, and Saint Gregory the Great—wrote extensively about their dream visions and considered dreams a gift from God.

It may seem strange that this valuable gift suddenly became something to be avoided. It appears that when Saint Jerome prepared the Vulgate Bible, which was based on a translation of Greek and Hebrew manuscripts, he deliberately mistranslated the Hebrew words for "witchcraft" and "soothsaying" on several occasions. Instead of writing "Thou shall not practice augury or witchcraft," Saint Jerome wrote "Thou shall not practice augury nor observe dreams."[29] Consequently, dreams ceased

---

29. Morton Kelsey, *God, Dreams and Revelation: A Christian Interpretation of Dreams* (Minneapolis: Augsburg, 1974). Originally published as *Dreams: The Dark Speech of the Spirit* (Garden City, NY: Doubleday, 1968).

to play an active role in spiritual work until the late twentieth century. The two people who rediscovered the value of Christian dreamwork were John Sanford and Morton Kelsey.[30]

When Muhammad (c. 570–632), the founder of Islam, was forty years old, he saw Gabriel in his dreams. Gabriel dictated the Koran to him in a series of visions, and the religion of Islam began.

Angels have appeared to people in dreams in more recent times also. One famous example was when the angel Moroni appeared to Joseph Smith (1805–1844) in a dream and told him where the golden tablets were buried. This event led to the establishment of the Church of Jesus Christ of Latter-day Saints.

Everybody dreams. Some people claim never to remember their dreams, but this is because people vary enormously in how much they remember them. Most dreams occur toward the end of the sleeping cycle, and these are quickly forgotten when people are woken by an alarm clock and have to leap out of bed and get ready for the day ahead. Fortunately, everybody can improve their recall of their dreams if they want to.

Remembering your dreams can be useful in many ways. Often, dreams relate to matters that are occurring in your life, and you can gain valuable insights into how you should handle a particular situation. Recurring dreams are highly significant and often relate to unresolved issues from the past. Precognitive

---

30. Morton Kelsey wrote *God, Dreams and Revelation: A Christian Interpretation of Dreams* (see note 29). John A. Sanford is author of *Dreams: God's Forgotten Language* (Philadelphia: Lippincott, 1968).

dreams provide valuable insights into the future. Many people experience healing dreams in which an angel appears to them in a dream to tell them they have been healed or to give advice on how they can heal themselves.

You can also request specific dreams before you fall asleep. Sometimes you will remember these dreams when you wake up, but even if you don't, you will have the answer to your request in your mind.

How to Sleep Better

To ensure pleasant dreams, and good dream recall, you need to enjoy a good night's sleep. People vary enormously in the amount of sleep they require, but most people need between seven and nine hours of sleep every night. A good friend of mine manages perfectly well on just four hours of sleep a night, but I need eight hours. Everyone is different.

Maintaining a regular schedule will help ensure you get the amount of sleep that you require. Moderate exercise two or three hours before you go to bed may help you enjoy a better night's sleep. If you find it difficult to get to sleep, avoid alcohol and caffeinated drinks late in the day. Relaxing in a warm bath before going to bed helps many people fall asleep more easily. I find reading a book in bed helps me unwind and relax.

Most people experience four or five dream periods every night. The first dream period starts about ninety minutes after falling asleep and lasts for ten to twenty minutes. This is followed by about ninety minutes of deeper sleep before another dream period begins. When you awaken naturally, it will be from a dream period.

Consequently, the best times to evaluate your dreams are when you wake up normally, with no pressing demands on your time. Lie quietly in bed without changing your position, and allow the memories of the dream to come back. Once you have explored the dream thoroughly and have recalled all the details you need, write everything down in a dream diary.

My dream diary is an exercise book I keep beside my bed. I recall as many of my dreams in it as possible. If I wake up in the middle of the night after a dream, I'll write down the main points. Doing so helps me recall the entire dream when I wake up in the morning, and I'll be able to expand on what I wrote during the night.

Keeping a dream diary is useful. It forces you to think about your dreams and to pay attention to them. Your dream diary also becomes more and more valuable as time goes on. You will find different themes cropping up again and again in your dreams. Obviously, you need to pay special attention to them.

Keeping a dream diary may not seem helpful if you find it hard to remember your dreams. In fact, the opposite is the case. The mere fact of keeping pen and paper beside your bed to preserve your dreams puts a strong focus on your dreams, and you are more likely to remember them.

Once you start paying attention to your dreams, you will sometimes wake up knowing you've been dreaming, but find it hard to bring the dream back into your mind. If you have moved, return to the position you were lying in when you first woke up. Lie quietly and see what memories come back. Often an image or thought will come to your mind, and this will unlock the entire dream. I find it helpful to try to recall the first thought I had when I woke up. This often leads me back into the dream. There is no need to worry if the dream fails to return. Allow about five minutes, and then get up. If the dream is important, you will experience it again, and you may be able to capture it then.

You are the best interpreter of your dreams. Dreams often speak in symbols that are personal to you. These symbolize what is going on in your life, and you may have to think about them for a while to understand what they mean. You can sometimes fail to gain the important message of a dream if you interpret it literally.

Dreams serve a valuable purpose in communicating between the physical and nonphysical worlds, which is why dreams are so useful in angelic communication. In the Bible, there are many examples of how God used His angels to communicate with humans through their dreams.

Dreamwork

Dreamwork is a process that uses your conscious imagination to make sense of the subconscious messages of your dreams. It is a fascinating exercise that will surprise you with the insights it uncovers. All you do in dreamwork is sit down quietly somewhere during the day, recall part of a dream, and then use your imagination to see where else it can take you. It is identical to the process that Dante went through during his three days and nights in purgatory. Every day he thought about the dream he had had the night before.

The process is deceptively simple, and some people find it hard to enter the right state of mind when they first start practicing dreamwork. Here is the process in detail:

1. Sit down comfortably, somewhere where you will not be interrupted for at least fifteen minutes.

2. Close your eyes, take several slow deep breaths, and relax.

3. Recapture part of a recent dream. Do not force a memory to come back. Sit quietly and wait for a memory to return.

4. When a memory comes to you, visualize it as clearly as you can, and follow it if it decides to go somewhere. Spend as long as you wish at this stage. If a number of characters or animals appear in your dream, you might want to follow each of them individually to see where it takes you.

5. Ask yourself what you feel in your body as you watch the dream. You may feel a definite sensation in part of your body. This is where your dream feels most comfortable. These are most likely to be in one of the chakra centers, which are energy centers in your aura. If you feel a sensation at the base of your spine, the energy relates to survival. The energy relates to sex if it is felt between the genitals and the navel. Just above the navel relates to power. If the energy is in the region of the heart, it relates to love. A sensation in the throat relates to self-expression. If it is felt in the region of the third

eye, it relates to wisdom and intuition. Finally, if it is felt at the top of your head, it relates to spirituality.

6. Experience the sensation for as long as you can and then ask for a message that will help you understand why your dream has chosen that particular place in your body.

7. Ask that part of your body for its reaction to the dream.

8. Ask your guardian angel to help you gain further insights into the dream. Visualize your guardian angel playing an active role in your dream.

9. Using your imagination, take the dream anywhere you wish to go. Ask your guardian angel for any further insights he can provide.

10. Thank your guardian angel. Take five slow, deep breaths and open your eyes.

11. Think about what you have experienced for a few minutes before getting up.

12. As soon as possible, write down everything that occurred.

Dreamwork can help you uncover different layers of your dream. Sometimes our dreams seem to make absolutely no sense at all, and this exercise is a good one to help clarify the messages the dream is trying to impart.

Guardian Angel Request

This is a simple exercise that involves asking your guardian angel to help you to resolve a problem or difficulty. Before going to bed, write a brief letter to your guardian angel. Seal it in an envelope and place it under your pillow. Just before falling asleep, silently thank your guardian angel for everything he does for you and ask for an answer to your problem.

When you wake up in the morning, you are likely to have an answer, usually through a dream. Sometimes the answer appears as a thought. If the answer has not arrived, go through your day in your normal manner. Often the answer will come to you when you least expect it. If you have not received an answer by the end of the day, write the same letter to your guardian angel again, and place this under your pillow. Repeat this until you have received a reply.

You need to remain alert, as sometimes the answers won't be what you want to hear. One of my students wrote a letter to her guardian angel asking for help in resolving a problem she had with a neighbor. The reply she received was to make friends with this person. This was not the answer she wanted, so she wrote the letter again, only to receive the same answer. After doing this several times, she finally gave up and visited the neighbor. To her amazement, she discovered the person was much more pleasant than she had thought, and they are now good friends.

Dream Messages

There is no need to wait until you have difficulties in your life to contact angels in your dreams. Before drifting off to sleep, you can ask the angels for their blessing and protection while you are asleep. This has two benefits. You will sleep better. This alone is a major benefit for many people. In addition, you may wake up in the morning with a clear message from the angelic realms. This message might be a keyword, a phrase, or even an entire message that will relate to what is going on in your life at the time.

The Angel Guardians of Sleep

Most people are not aware of their guardian angel while they are awake. Still fewer know that their guardian angel watches over them while they are asleep. In our dreams, we frequently encounter angels. Men recognize the feminine side of the angels they meet in their dreams, while women interact with the male energies of the angels they encounter. It is not uncommon to encounter companies of angels in our dreams, either. However, our personal guardian angel is always present and instantly recognizable, even in our dreams.

The angel guardians of sleep look over us while we rest. They also provide us with symbols in our dreams. Many people find it hard to recognize and understand the symbology of their dreams. However, by recording them and seeing what happens later, it is possible to learn how to use these symbols and make good use of them. They provide warnings and intimations about future events, our health, our motivation, and our general well-being.

Mantras and Angels

Mantras are brief phrases that are repeated over and over. Some of my students have called these "affirmations with the angels," and this is as good an explanation as any. To make use of these mantras or affirmations, you need to compose a suitable phrase that you can repeat as many times as possible while you are falling asleep. The idea is that your guardian angel will hear your mantra and act on it while you are resting.

You can use your mantras at any time, but the most effective time to say them is while you are falling asleep. This ensures that the angels will work on them while you rest. I also find that repeating my mantras helps me fall asleep more easily on long plane rides. If you repeat your mantras during the day, you might be able to say them out loud. This is especially useful, as you hear yourself saying them. However, when you are lying in bed waiting for sleep, it is better to say them silently, confident that your guardian angel will receive the message.

The words you use are entirely up to you. Some people use Bible quotes, such as "I can do all things through Jesus Christ who strengtheneth me." Others create mantras of their own, such as "My desire and God's desire are exactly the same" and "I attract wealth and happiness everywhere I go." You can use standard affirmations as well. One I sometimes use while waiting in line at the bank is: "I create wealth and abundance." You can also create mantras to cover a temporary situation. If you are concerned about someone, you might use "May the angels surround [person's name] with love and protection." Mantras make an effective way of helping others. They need not be directed solely at you and your needs.

Lucid Dreaming

Lucid dreaming is the term used to describe a dream in which you realize you are dreaming while still in the dream. Most people experience lucid dreams occasionally, but few take the trouble to learn how to create them at will.

The first person to experiment with lucid dreaming was a nineteenth-century French professor of Chinese literature named Marquis d'Hervey de Saint-Denys. He started recording his dreams at the age of thirteen and ultimately wrote a book called *Dreams and How to Guide Them*.[31]

Not everyone approved of his findings, and when the Dutch physician Frederik Willems van Eeden decided to write a book on the subject, his first thought was to express his ideas in the form of a novel, as they would be less controversial if presented in that form. He never wrote the novel, nor the book he hoped to write on the subject, but in 1913 he presented a paper on the subject to the British Society for Psychical Research in which he introduced the term "lucid dreaming."

When you are dreaming and become aware that you are dreaming, you have the ability to take the dream wherever you wish it to go. You might choose to visit a favorite place or see a friend. You might want to go forward or backward through history. You might choose to meet your guardian angel or any other member of the angelic kingdom.

Lucid dreaming is not hard to do, but it can sometimes be difficult to have a lucid dream on request. I have found it best to tell myself in a casual fashion before going to bed that I will have a lucid dream. If I insist or demand that I experience a

---

31. Marquis d'Hervey de Saint-Denys, *Dreams and How to Guide Them*, trans. Nicholas Fry (London: Duckworth, 1982). Originally published in 1867 in French as *Les rêves et les moyens de les diriger*.

lucid dream, it seldom occurs. Here are the steps to achieving a lucid dream:

1. Lie in bed and casually tell yourself that you will have a lucid dream. Decide on a particular action that will take you directly into a lucid dream. If you have a recurring dream, tell yourself that the next time you dream this particular dream, you will become aware of the fact and immediately enter into a lucid dream. You might tell yourself that whenever you see your hand during the course of a dream, it will be a message to your mind that you are about to lucid dream.

2. Once you become aware that you are lucid dreaming, tell yourself that you wish to meet your guardian angel. You will immediately find yourself in front of him. One big advantage of lucid dreaming is that you can become as close as you wish to any situation. If a scene is emotionally difficult, for instance, you can take a few steps back, or even leave the situation entirely.

3. Converse with your guardian angel. Ask him any questions you wish. Ask him to take you to places or situations that will benefit you. Ask him if you are praying as effectively as you could be. Ask him for any favors or blessings that you wish for yourself or others. Once you have completed the conversation, thank your guardian angel and allow yourself to return to your bed.

4. Visualize yourself tucked up in your own bed. See yourself lying peacefully in a state of deep repose, and allow yourself to drift back into sleep.

5. Record everything you can remember when you wake up in the morning.

Conscious Dreaming

Lucid dreaming is a useful skill, one that I believe everyone can learn. However, even skilled lucid dreamers find it difficult to enter the lucid state on request. Fortunately, conscious dreaming is similar, and frequently turns into a lucid dream.

It is important that you do not overindulge in food, drink, or other stimulants before going to bed. Here is the process:

1. Go to bed at your normal time, and think of your desire to have a meeting with your guardian angel or whomever else you wish to contact.

2. Consciously relax all the muscles of your body. Let your thoughts flow freely, but keep them as positive as possible. If you find yourself thinking any negative thoughts, deliberately let them go. Tell yourself that you'll worry about that concern tomorrow, and start thinking of something positive.

3. When you feel completely relaxed, start thinking of different experiences you have had in your life, and visualize the surroundings as well as the occurrences. Start with a recent event and gradually go back through your life as far as you can.

4. While doing this, you may be captivated by one of the experiences. Explore this situation in as much detail as you wish. Visualize yourself inside the scene, walking around a corner and meeting your guardian angel.

Once you have made this connection, you can both go somewhere comfortable to relax and enjoy a pleasant conversation.

5. If none of the scenes leads you into a meeting with your guardian angel, continue going back as far as you can. When you cannot remember any earlier experiences, ask your guardian angel to take you somewhere where you can chat.

6. In both cases, enjoy the conversation for as long as you wish. Finally, thank him and say good night before visualizing yourself returning to your bed and falling asleep.

Frequently, this exercise will lead you into a lucid dream. If this occurs, you might be able to make other explorations and discoveries before returning to your bed. In practice, though, I usually find myself sound asleep before completing all the things I had intended to do.

Dreaming is a highly effective way of communicating with the angelic kingdom. However, some people find it frustrating, as they do not always remember what happened in the course of their dreams. Fortunately, there is a method of communicating with angels that is more straightforward and direct. We will look at this in the next chapter.

NINE

Dowsing for Angels

Dowsing is the art of finding something that is hidden. People frequently dowse with a pendulum to find water, oil, lost objects, and missing people. Dowsing can be used to determine the health of plants, animals, and people. It can also help people develop physically, mentally, emotionally, and even spiritually. The pendulum is a wonderful tool, and I'm constantly surprised that more people do not make use of it.

A pendulum is a small weight suspended on a length of thread, chain, or cord. When I was growing up, my mother frequently dowsed using her wedding ring attached to a length of thread. You can buy attractive pendulums at New Age stores, but any small weight attached to thread or chain works just as well. You might like to experiment with impromptu pendulums before buying one. I have a huge collection of pendulums, as my children often buy me a small object attached to a chain as Christmas and birthday presents.

The ideal pendulum is one that weighs about three ounces, is attractive to look at, and is comfortable to use. Pendulums that are round in shape and have a point at the bottom are the easiest to use and are generally well-balanced and sensitive. The thread or chain should be four or five inches long, although some people prefer it longer.

Most people use the pendulum with the hand they write with. However, it is also worth experimenting with the other hand, as you may find that it works better for you.

Start by sitting at a table, with the elbow of the arm that is holding the pendulum resting on the table. This elbow should be the only part of your body in contact with the table. Hold the thread or chain of the pendulum between your thumb and index finger, with the palm of this hand facing downwards. Place your feet firmly on the ground. The pendulum should be about a foot in front of you.

Start by gently swinging the pendulum from side to side to become familiar with its movements. Swing it in different directions, and then swing it in gentle circles, both clockwise and counterclockwise. Experiment with holding the thread or chain in different places, creating a longer or shorter length.

Once you have become used to the pendulum's movements, stop the pendulum with your free hand. When it is still, ask which movement indicates a positive, or "yes," response. You can ask this question silently or out loud. If you have not used a pendulum before, it might take a minute or two to respond. It will probably make a small movement at first, but the movements will become stronger with practice. The pendulum will move from side to side, towards and away from you, or in circles, either clockwise or counterclockwise.

When the pendulum gives you a "yes" response, stop its movements with your free hand, and ask for the negative, or "no," response. Once you have this, you can continue by asking for the "I don't know" and "I don't want to answer" responses.

Now that you have the four possible responses, you can start asking your pendulum questions. Start by asking questions that you already know the answers for. You might ask: "Am I male?" You should get a positive response if you are, and a negative response if you aren't. You can follow this up by asking similar questions about your age, occupation, marital status, number of children, and so on.

The purpose of this is to get you used to the pendulum and to demonstrate its accuracy. Once you have achieved this, you can start asking questions that you do not know the answers to, but can confirm later. Again, you will find the pendulum to be highly accurate.

There is one proviso to this, though. If you have an emotional involvement in the outcome of the question, your mind will overrule the pendulum and give you the answer you want.

If, for instance, someone close to you is pregnant and you're using the pendulum to determine the sex of the unborn child, the pendulum will give you the correct answer if you genuinely don't care what sex the baby will be. However, if you hope it will be a girl, for instance, the pendulum will also tell you it will be a girl, even if this proves not to be the case. Whenever you have an emotional interest in the outcome it is better to ask someone with no personal interest in the answer to dowse for you.

You need to phrase your questions carefully. The pendulum cannot respond to: "Should I contact Raphael or Michael?" In this instance, you could ask the question twice, once for each archangel.

It is often better to ask a series of simple questions rather than one all-encompassing question. Most problems can be handled by your guardian angel, but if it relates to a specific topic, you might consider contacting one of the angels who has a special interest in that matter. You might ask: "Should I contact my guardian angel about this concern?" If the answer is positive, you should tell your guardian angel about your problem and ask him to help you deal with it. You may find the pendulum gives you a negative response. If this occurs, you can ask: "Is [name of angel] the right angel for me to contact about my problem?" You could ask this question about as many angels as you wish until you receive a positive response.

Angel Pendulum

You can use any type of pendulum to contact the angels. However, angels respond especially well to crystals, and a crystal pendulum that you use only for communicating with angels would be the perfect choice. A clear crystal pendulum attached to a length of attractive chain or cord is not only pleasing to handle and look at, but will gradually become more and more attuned to you and your guardian angel as you work with it.

The crystal can be anything that is pleasing to you. I have a number of crystal pendulums, and the one I use especially for working with the angels is selenite. Selenite is a translucent white crystal that glows with a special radiance when polished. It is often used for protection, and also helps people to think, concentrate, and grow inwardly. It can be used to contact any angel, but has a special bond with Archangel Gabriel.

Another possibility is celestite, which comes in a variety of colors from white through to brown. It helps you to receive messages from the angels clairaudiently (receiving the message as thoughts in your head).

Rutilated quartz is another popular choice. It is sometimes called "angel hair," as the inclusions of fine rutile look like strands of hair that have been trapped inside the crystal. Quartz amplifies any communications you have with the angels, making it easier to both send and receive messages.

Spiritual Growth and Development

You can use the pendulum to help in your spiritual growth in many ways. You can ask it about specific churches, faiths, and religions. Not long ago, I asked my pendulum if I should attend a rally put on by a Christian evangelist who was visiting my city. I was surprised to receive a positive response, but went, and learned a great deal in the course of the evening. I tend to avoid gatherings of that sort, and would not have considered going if my pendulum had not given the response it did.

Here is an interesting experiment you can perform at any time. Hold your pendulum and say: "I am divine love. I am universal love. I am a spiritual being. I am."

Your pendulum should give a positive response to these words. However, if your pendulum fails to react, or gives a negative response, you should repeat the words several times a day as an affirmation. After a few days, test the words with your pendulum again. Keep on doing this until you receive a positive response.

You can test any words or phrases in the same way. Here are some suggestions:

I am happy.

I am a good person.

I express love and goodwill to everyone I meet.

I am generous and kind.

I deserve the best that life has to offer.

I am divine spirit.

Dowsing with the Angels

Your pendulum will become more and more useful as you get used to it. You can involve the angels in all your dowsing sessions by inviting the angels to assist. You can do this by performing a ritual beforehand. Alternatively, you might want to ask the pendulum: "Do I have the angels' blessing on the questions I'm going to ask?" A positive response to this question will assure you that the angels are present, and will provide you with all the help and support you may require.

Obviously, if you receive a negative response, you should ask further questions to establish why they are not prepared to bless your session with the pendulum. There could be a number of reasons why this might happen. You might be inadvertently overlooking other people's needs, in which case your questions will not necessarily benefit everyone concerned.

You may find the angels think you should work out the answer on your own without using your pendulum. This occurs every now and again, as many people become carried away with the pendulum and use it excessively, asking it about everything that is going on in their lives.

I usually carry a pendulum with me. However, I may not use it for several weeks. In practice, I use it only when I am unable to determine an answer on my own. Consequently, I might use the pendulum several times in one week, and then not use it for a month or two. It's a valuable tool that I do not hesitate to use, but I don't want it to become a crutch.

Your Guardian Angel and the Pendulum

Your guardian angel is ready to help you at any time. However, if you have a number of questions, you may want to set aside a special time for a longer conversation. You can do this by asking the pendulum if now is a good time to communicate with your guardian angel. Almost always, the answer will be yes, but occasionally your request will be declined. You need to accept this, as there will be an important reason for it. You might be overly anxious, stressed, or angry, for instance, and your guardian angel might want you to calm down before having a conversation.

If the pendulum tells you that it is a good time to have a conversation, you can continue asking questions with your pendulum, or perform a ritual to communicate with him directly.

Learning Your Guardian Angel's Name

If you have not discovered your guardian angel's name in the course of previous conversations, you can learn it from the pendulum. You do this by going through the alphabet one letter at a time to determine the first letter of the name. Repeat as many times as necessary to learn his full name.

Multi-choice Questions

Your guardian angel can help you decide on the right choice from several possibilities. Friends of mine recently decided to celebrate their twenty-fifth wedding anniversary in one of their favorite cities in Europe. As they loved many European cities, they found it hard to decide on one. I suggested they write each destination on a separate slip of paper, and ask their guardian angels to select the perfect city for their celebration using the pendulum. The guardian angels selected Barcelona, and they had a wonderful time revisiting their favorite places in that beautiful city.

You can ask your guardian angel to help you select the right car, the right job, career, home, and anything else that has a number of choices. A young friend recently bought himself a used car this way. He selected several cars from newspaper advertisements and then asked his guardian angel to determine, through the pendulum, which one would be best for him. By doing this, he saved a great deal of time and ended up with a good, reliable vehicle.

Self-improvement Cards

Your guardian angel has your best interests at heart and will do everything possible to help you progress in this incarnation. Naturally, your guardian angel will be delighted if you start focusing on areas of your life that need improvement. With the help of your guardian angel, your pendulum, and a pack of file cards, you can start moving ahead today.

Start by writing down the qualities you would like to develop on separate file cards. I prefer to write phrases, but some people prefer to use a single word that sums up the essence of the quality they wish to develop. Here are some possibilities that might apply to you:

Express the love I feel

Unlimited confidence

Patience

Self-expression

Tolerance

Compassion

Express enthusiasm

Accept abundance

Express joy and happiness

Study, and grow in knowledge and wisdom

Listen

Integrity

Strength

Gratitude

Think before talking

Trust my intuition

Develop spiritually

Focus on my goals

Let go of the past

Exercise regularly

You can add to your list whenever you wish. There are a number of ways in which you can use the cards. You might want to spread them out on a table and ask your guardian angel to tell you, through the pendulum, which quality you should work on today. Hold the pendulum over each card in turn, and see which one your guardian angel selects.

Alternatively, you might like to mix the cards and place them face down on the table. Again, ask your guardian angel to select one of the cards for you. A similar method is to mix the cards and hold them in a pile face down. Ask your guardian angel to help you select a suitable quality by choosing a number. A number may pop into your mind, or you could use your pendulum to choose a number for you. You do this by suspending your pendulum inside a drinking glass and asking your guardian angel to reveal the number. The pendulum will start moving and will tap the side of the glass a number of times to indicate the number. Count down to that number card in the stack of cards, and work on that particular quality.

Once you have chosen the quality to work on, carry that card around with you for the rest of the day. Every time you see the card, it will remind you of your goal.

At the end of the day, you can ask your guardian angel to review your progress. Suspend your pendulum over the card and ask your guardian angel questions that will clarify how you got on. You should ask your guardian angel if you should work with the card for another day. Keep on working with the particular quality until your guardian angel gives a negative reply to this question. When that happens, you can use the pendulum to help you select another quality to work on.

The pendulum is based on a subconscious ideomotor response, which enables the pendulum to move. The mind acts on an idea and causes minuscule physical responses that move the pendulum. Automatic writing works on the same principle and enables you to communicate with your angels at an even deeper level. We will look at this in the next chapter.

TEN

Automatic Writing

Automatic writing is writing produced without any conscious effort or thought. The person holding the pen allows the instrument to move freely while some other power or agent takes control. Frequently, this person can watch television or engage in conversation at the same time as the hand is writing. Some automatic writers enter into a trance state, but most remain fully aware of everything that is going on around them.

Automatic writing is an extremely pleasant way to gain insights and knowledge. It is stimulating, exciting, and completely effortless.

Sometimes the pen will move rapidly for an hour or more, yet the person will feel just as fresh at the end as he or she did at the start. Geraldine Cummins (1890–1969), a well-known Irish medium who wrote fifteen books using automatic writing, was able to write at almost two thousand words an hour.[32]

Although automatic writing sometimes produces gibberish, it can also produce amazing results that are well beyond the conscious ability or knowledge of the person holding the pen. Many religious works have been written with automatic writing. This even includes parts of the Bible: "And there came a writing to him from Elijah the prophet, saying . . ." (II Chronicles 21:12).

Most of the time, automatic writing is produced much more quickly than conscious writing. The script is usually larger than what the person would use normally. Frederick W. H. Myers (1843–1901), the British psychic researcher, even found someone who could write different messages simultaneously, using a planchette in each hand.[33]

Automatic writing has had some amazing successes. Andrew Jackson Davis (1826–1910), the American seer and phi-

---

32. *The ESP Reader*, ed. David C. Knight (New York: Grosset and Dunlop, 1969), 235. The best-known books by Geraldine Cummins are *The Scripts of Cleophas, Paul in Athens, The Great Days of Ephesus, The Road to Immortality, They Survive, Unseen Adventures, Mind in Life and Death,* and *Swan on a Black Sea.*

33. A planchette is a small heart-shaped piece of wood with three legs. Two of the legs are on wheels, and the third leg contains a pencil. The fingertips of one hand rests on the top of the device, which can then move freely, creating words and pictures. Monsieur M. Planchette, a French spiritualist, is credited with inventing them in the middle of the nineteenth century. Planchettes are still available, but were superseded by the popularity of the Ouija board.

losopher, wrote his most important work, *The Principles of Nature, Her Divine Revelations, and a Voice to Mankind* using automatic writing. The book was published in 1847, and played a major role in the growth of spiritualism.

Harriet Beecher Stowe (1811–1896), author of *Uncle Tom's Cabin*, said of the book that made her famous: "I didn't write it; it was given to me. It passed before me."

William Blake (1757–1827), the famous English poet who regularly saw angels, wrote in his preface to the poem *Jerusalem* that it had been dictated to him. "The grandest poem that this world contains; I may praise it, since I dare not pretend to be other than the Secretary; the authors are in eternity," he wrote.

André Breton (1896–1966), the French poet and leader of the Surrealist movement, produced several works using automatic writing. The most famous of these is *Soluble Fish*.

Automatic writing enabled Frederick Bligh Bond (1864–1945) to locate the lost Edgar and Loretto Chapels at Glastonbury Abbey. Bond asked a friend, John Allen Bartlett, who was an experienced automatic writer, to help. The messages that came through were in a mixture of Latin and Old English and came from an entity called "Gulielmus Monachus," or "William the Monk." The Anglican Church was thrilled with the discovery, but were embarrassed when Bond wrote a book called *The Gate of Remembrance*[34] that described how he had found the Edgar Chapel. Five years later, Frederick Bligh Bond was forced to resign and the excavations ceased.

---

34. Frederick Bligh Bond, *The Gate of Remembrance: The Story of the Psychological Experiment Which Resulted in the Discovery of the Edgar Chapel at Glastonbury* (Oxford: B. H. Blackwell, 1918).

Probably the most famous example of automatic writing is the huge volume of work produced by a discarnate being called Patience Worth, who began communicating with two friends, Pearl Curran and Emily Hutchinson, in 1913. They were experimenting with a Ouija board when a message was spelled out: "Many moons ago I lived. Again I come. Patience Worth is my name." Over the next five years, Patience Worth dictated more than four million words. These included twenty-five hundred poems, as well as short stories, plays, epigrams, and six novels. Her works enjoyed critical acclaim, and her first two novels, *The Sorry Tale* and *Hope Trueblood*, became bestsellers. Eventually, the sheer volume of words that came through encouraged the women to find a more convenient method. In 1920, Pearl Curran found she could dictate the words as they came to her in automatic speech.

First Steps in Automatic Writing

Automatic writing is a skill that anyone can develop. In fact, if you have ever doodled a design or picture, you have already practiced a form of automatic writing.

Automatic writing takes practice. Most people start by producing shapes and scribbles, then move on to produce words, sentences, and ultimately, in some cases, books. You will need a large pad of paper and a good quality pen or pencil. I like to use a soft lead pencil of good quality and an artist's sketch pad. You will also need a quiet place where you can practice without being disturbed.

The most important requirement is peace of mind. If you are upset or angry when you start automatic writing, your pen is likely to pick up a low-level spirit or entity. Automatic writing sometimes reveals insights from the person's subconscious mind. If you practice when you are feeling low, you are likely to uncover unwanted memories and feelings. Ideally, you should be feeling positive about your life. The best time to practice automatic writing is in the evening, as tiredness seems to help the process.

1. Place the pad on a table and sit beside it with your pen in your hand resting on the paper. Your elbow should form a right angle.

2. Mentally surround yourself with protective white light. If you have a specific angel you want to communicate with, ask for him by name. If you are leaving it to chance, ensure that you ask for positive angels.

3. Distract yourself in some way. I like to look out a window and go into a daydream. You might prefer to watch television or listen to the radio.

4. Do not look at the pad of paper or the hand holding the pen. Allow the pen to move as it wishes. If nothing happens after a few minutes, ask the hand holding the pen if it has any messages for you.

5. Distract yourself again, and allow the pen to move if it wants to. If nothing happens after another few minutes, give up for the day.

6. Keep calm when the pen starts to move. Many people feel startled the first time this happens, and ruin it by focusing on what the pen is doing. If you accidentally do this, put a fresh sheet of paper under your pen and start again.

7. Practice at the same time every day until you achieve success.

8. You first attempts are unlikely to produce valuable insights. You are more likely to produce scribbles and shapes, such as circles and ovals, than coherent sentences. Even when you start writing words, they may not make any sense to begin with. Consider these successes, as they show you are on the right track.

Introducing the Angels

Once you have mastered automatic writing, you can use it for different purposes. You can consciously write down questions and receive the answers to them through automatic writing. It is important that you have no emotional attachment to the answer, as when this occurs you are likely to receive the answer you want rather than the correct reply. Automatic writing is similar to pendulum dowsing in this respect.

You can also communicate with the angelic kingdom with automatic writing. You will need a pen, paper, and at least one white candle. Here is the procedure:

I. Create a Circle of Protection around you.

2. Light the candle(s).

3. Write a letter to a specific angel. You can write this letter in advance if you wish. I prefer to think about it ahead of time, and then write it while inside the circle. Fold the letter and place it in an envelope. Seal it and write the angel's name on the front.

4. Hold the sealed envelope high in the air for a few moments. Kiss it, and then "mail" the message by burning the envelope in the flame of the candle.

5. Sit quietly beside your altar or table and wait for the angel you are communicating with to reply using automatic writing. Pay no attention to what your hand is doing until you are certain the message has been fully received.

6. Put the pen down and thank the angel for the reply. Read the message from the angel and, if necessary, ask more questions until you have received a complete answer.

7. Snuff out the candle(s) and close the circle.

8. Have something to eat and drink before reading the message.

Automatic writing is a useful skill that will help you communicate with any angel you wish. Some people take to it naturally and gain valuable insights almost from the start. Most people need both time and patience to develop their ability at automatic writing. However, it is like riding a bicycle. Once you've mastered it, you'll have a useful tool that you can use whenever you wish for the rest of your life.

Automatic Dictation

Automatic dictation is related to automatic writing. The difference is that the angels talk to you, and you then consciously write their answers down. Some people find this easier to do than automatic writing. The process is similar.

1. Create a Circle of Protection.

2. Sit down comfortably inside the circle with a pen and a pad of paper.

3. Recite the Lord's Prayer or read a page or two from a spiritual book. Doing so helps you reach the correct state of mind for the experiment.

4. Ask for a specific angel to come and talk with you. You can ask silently or out loud.

5. Wait patiently until you hear a voice. This voice usually appears as thoughts in your mind. However, you may also hear a voice.

6. Confirm that the angel is the one you wanted to communicate with. Welcome the angel and thank him for coming.

7. Ask a question. Listen carefully to the answer, and consciously write it down.

8. Continue asking questions until you have covered everything you wished to with the angel.

9. Thank the angel and say goodbye. Close down the Circle of Protection and carry on with your day.

10. Later, when you have free time, read the answers again and act on them.

We have covered a wide variety of angels in the course of this book. People sometimes find it hard to determine which angel they should contact for a specific purpose. Choosing the correct angel is the subject of the next chapter.

The Right Angel
for the Right Situation

The angels are willing and prepared to help you in every type of situation. However, it is not always easy to determine which angel you should call on for a specific purpose. Your first choice should usually be your guardian angel, but there will be times when you need additional, possibly more specialized help. If you are in danger, for instance, you should call on Archangel Michael for help and protection. I hope you will never need to call on him for that purpose, but you never know when you might find yourself in a difficult situation. I have needed instant help several times over the years, and Michael always came to my aid the moment I called out to him.

If you were about to go mountain climbing, you might call on Adnachiel for assistance, as he enjoys helping people engaged in adventurous pursuits. Likewise, if you were having problems with your teenage children, you might call on Afriel, who enjoys working with young people. An acquaintance of mine has just opened up a small retail shop. She frequently calls on Anauel, as he is one of the angels concerned with prosperity and financial success.

There are angels for every possible purpose. If you are unsure which particular angel to call on, ask your guardian angel to put you in touch with the angel who is best suited for your needs.

Your Guardian Angel

Your guardian angel has been looking after you from the day you were born, constantly providing guidance, protection, support, and companionship.

You should call on your guardian angel whenever you face temptation. Usually, your guardian angel will suggest you do the right thing. You may not consciously be aware of it, as the message is likely to come as a flash of intuition.

You should call on your guardian angel whenever you pray. God will always receive your prayers, no matter how you say them. However, your guardian angel melds his prayers with yours, making them even more effective.

Your guardian angel constantly provides protection for you. You can always ask for additional protection whenever you do something that takes you out of your normal comfort zone. Taking a trip, or learning a new skill, are good examples.

EDWINA'S EXPERIENCE

Edwina came to several of my psychic development classes over the years. She was an extremely quiet and shy teenager when I first met her, and she spoke very little at the classes. This changed when we started studying angels.

"I always knew I had a guardian angel," she told me, "but I didn't know how to talk to him."

Every week after that, she'd tell us about her communications with her guardian angel. Most of these involved problems with her boyfriend, and her guardian angel always gave good advice.

After a few months, her guardian angel started warning her about her boyfriend, hinting that he led a double life and wasn't the person she thought he was. When she asked her boyfriend about this, he became angry and abusive. Edwina didn't know what to do. She thought she loved her boyfriend, but had now seen another side of his character. She trusted her guardian angel implicitly.

Members of the class made various suggestions to her, but it was Edwina who decided to end the relationship. Her boyfriend was furious, but there was nothing he could do about it.

Edwina went through a difficult period. She was lonely, and despite the assurances of her guardian angel, she wondered if she'd done the right thing.

The phone woke Edwina early one morning. It was a woman Edwina worked with in her part-time job. She told Edwina that her former boyfriend had been arrested on drug-dealing charges and was in prison.

Edwina visited him a few times. "My guardian angel suggested I do that," she told us. "In a way, it set me free, as he didn't want anything to do with me. Now I'm able to get on with my life. My guardian angel tells me there's a much better man waiting for me, and that it won't be long before I meet him."

Edwina communicates with her guardian angel at least twice a day. "We discuss everything," she told me. "We pray together, and he brings a whole new dimension to my prayers. I never used to pray before. I haven't contacted any other angels yet. There's been no need for that, as my guardian angel is happy to help me whenever I need it."

Angels of the Elements

You should call on the angels of the elements whenever you need to eliminate negativity from your life. Negativity comes from many directions. Sometimes we create it in our own minds, while at other times the negative comments, attitudes, and behavior of other people create a negative environment. Try to avoid negative people as much as you can. Life is easier, and much more enjoyable, when you spend time with fun-loving, positive people.

You should also call on the angels of the elements whenever you feel the need for their particular energies. If you need grounding, for instance, you should contact the angels of the earth. The angels of air will give you energy and eloquence. The angels of water restore your emotional equilibrium, and the angels of fire provide enthusiasm and a desire for knowledge.

TIMOTHY'S EXPERIENCE

When I first met Timothy, he was working as a laboratory technician in a large hospital. His secret dream was to make his living as a portrait artist. Few people outside of his family knew of his talent with paints, and even his family didn't know of his dream.

Timothy's life began to change when we discussed the angels of the elements in class. He started asking questions about the angels of water and whether they could help creativity. Usually, Timothy stayed behind after the class to enjoy a cup of tea or coffee and a chat with the other students. However, he left as soon as the class ended on the night we discussed the angels of the elements.

The following week, he told us of his dream, and how it had always seemed impossible.

"I might have a bit of talent," he told us, "but I've had no formal training. It seemed almost arrogant to think I could make money from my painting. But every night since I was last here, I conducted a ritual and spoke with the angels of water. They tell me to believe in myself, and they'll help me make it happen."

Some of the other members of the class were skeptical. "Don't you have a mortgage?" someone asked.

"Yes, I do. And a wife and two kids."

"Can you start part-time?" someone else asked.

Timothy nodded. "That's my plan. But the angels tell me I'll be doing it full-time before I know it."

The following week, Timothy brought in one of his portraits to show us. We were all amazed at how good it was, and one of the students spoke to him afterwards and ordered a portrait.

A few weeks later, Timothy spoke to us all again. "The angels say I'm not charging enough. So I've put my prices up."

Again, some of the students were dubious. "Wouldn't it be better to charge a small amount until you've built up a market?" someone asked.

Timothy shrugged. "It's what the angels tell me. I'm sure they're right."

They were. Timothy got more commissions, and quickly had a waiting list of people wanting their portraits painted. About five years after that, he phoned me in a state of great excitement.

"I'm about to give up my job. The angels tell me I can make a full-time living from my painting."

Angels of the Zodiac

You should call on your zodiacal angels whenever you are thinking about or planning your future. If you are thinking about someone else's future, you should use either their zodiacal angels or the angels of the month you happen to be in.

You can also use the angels for the days of the week, or the individual hours, for help at specific times.

The best time to contact your zodiacal angels is on your birthday. Ask them for suggestions and help for the year ahead. You can also make a specific request from them at this time.

HAMISH'S EXPERIENCE

I never met Hamish. His wife, Gladys, attended several of my classes and shared what she learned with Hamish every evening when she returned home. We happened to discuss the angels of the zodiac a week or so before Hamish's birthday.

Hamish decided to write a letter to his astrological angel. He went for a long walk to think about what he would ask for. He and Gladys had teenage children who were causing them constant stress and aggravation. Their older son was mixing with dubious company, and they were concerned he was becoming involved with drugs. Hamish was also having problems at work and had been considering looking for work in a different field. In addition to this, Hamish's elderly mother had broken her hip and needed frequent attention.

When he came back from his walk, Hamish wrote a letter and placed it under his pillow. When Gladys told him he was supposed to perform a ritual first, he told her that he'd already communed with the angel while he was out walking. He wouldn't tell her what he had asked for, either. When she came to class the next week, Gladys told us that he'd had several dreams about his request and had recorded them in a notebook. The following week, Gladys told us that Hamish had "mailed" his letter.

The course finished before Hamish received an answer to his request. I had completely forgotten about it when Gladys phoned me about three months later.

"You're not going to believe it," she told me. "Hamish and I are going to Brazil for three weeks!"

"Brazil?" I was surprised. I had never heard her mention travel before.

"Yes. That's what Hamish asked his angel for. He's always wanted to go to Rio de Janeiro."

I thought about all their other concerns. Gladys must have picked up on my thoughts. "My sister's moving in to look after the family while we're away, and Hamish's mother is now in a home."

"That's great," I replied. "I'm sure you'll have a fabulous time."

"You'll never guess where the money came from," Gladys continued. I had been wondering, but would never have asked. "Hamish brought in a big contract at his work, and they gave him a bonus. It's enough to cover the whole trip." Gladys laughed. "I can't wait for my birthday. I already know what to write in my letter!"

Angels of Healing

You can call on the angels of healing at any time. It is not necessary to wait until someone close to you needs physical healing. Call on the angels of healing whenever you feel stressed, overtired, or exhausted. Call on them to send love and healing to the special people in your life. You can even ask them to send healing to your pets and plants.

Catherine's Experience

Catherine was in her mid-seventies when I first met her. She was a sprightly lady with a permanent twinkle in her eyes. She took pride in her appearance and was always immaculately dressed. Because of her age, I was surprised when she told the class that she calling on the angels of healing to help her mother.

Catherine's mother was ninety-seven. She was in reasonable health and had reluctantly moved into a retirement home a few months earlier. She was unhappy there, and Catherine thought she had lost the will to live.

She conducted a ritual to contact her guardian angel, and asked him to contact her mother's guardian angel to see what healing she could send. Two nights later, she received a reply in her dreams. Her mother's guardian angel did not want any healing, but asked Catherine to ask Raphael to send her love.

Catherine was thrilled to receive a direct reply. She had hoped her ritual would work, but had not expected to hear anything from her mother's guardian angel. Later that day, she created a magic circle and had a lengthy conversation with Raphael. That night she had the best sleep she'd had in years.

Naturally, everyone in the class wanted to know more.

"It's hard to say, really," Catherine told us. "I know my mother is much happier in the home. She always used to complain about it, and that's stopped. The biggest difference is the interest she has in what's going on in the world. She always used to keep up with the news, and I was sad when she lost interest, as it seemed like a step downward. Now she's reading the newspaper and watching the news on TV again. One of the nurses told me she's taking short walks. She's limited in her movements, so I know they must be very short walks, but it's good all the same. Her appetite has come back, too." Catherine beamed. "I have no doubts at all that Raphael is sending her plenty of love."

Every time Catherine performed a ritual, she thanked Raphael for his help. Catherine's mother lived for another two years, then died peacefully in her sleep.

"I'm sure Raphael came and told me her time was up," Catherine told me. "I woke up in the morning absolutely surrounded by love. I couldn't recapture my dream, but I know Raphael must have been in it. I had just got out of bed when the phone rang. Of course, I knew what it was before I answered it. After speaking to the nurse, I contacted Raphael and thanked him for making the last two years of my mother's life so happy for both of us."

Angels of Abundance

You can call on the angels of abundance at any time, but strangely it is best to call on them when you're feeling positive about your life. When you're feeling upbeat, happy, and motivated, you're more likely to listen, absorb, and act on the suggestions the angels of abundance give you.

Naturally, you can still call on them when you are feeling sad or impoverished, but be aware that you will need to be vigilant and aware in order to accept and act on the advice they give you.

Victor's Experience

I sometimes wondered why Victor came to my classes. He was a highly successful businessman who owned a chain of women's fashion stores. Every now and again, I saw photographs of him and his glamorous wife in the gossip pages of our Sunday newspaper. I gradually learned more about him from the conversations we had after the classes. He owned houses in two countries, collected antique cars, and traveled regularly. It seemed he was living the perfect life.

Victor was quiet in the class, but took pages of notes every week. Occasionally, he would ask a question, but he seldom contributed when class members were invited to share their experiences. Consequently, I was surprised when he arrived back at class after a seven-week overseas vacation and asked if he could speak about his experience with the angels of abundance.

"I was surprised to discover the angels of abundance," Victor told us. "I thought hard work and dedication were all that mattered. I've been very fortunate financially, and thought I knew all about abundance." He shook his head. "Not true. I have a better idea now though."

He proceeded to tell us about his two sons, twins aged twenty-five. "I was too hard on them from the outset," he confessed. "I had to work hard when I was young, and I thought I'd be giving them good work habits. Unfortunately, nothing they did was ever good enough for me. I forgot they were only kids. I gave them all the material things you could ever dream of, but I never gave them what they really wanted—my love." Victor briefly looked as if he was going to cry, but swallowed and kept on talking. "Kathy kept telling me, but I knew better. Then one Christmas, six years ago, Dave and Joel disappeared. They were both at college and living at home. One night they were home; next morning they'd gone. They kept in touch with Kathy, so we knew they were all right. They'd left because I didn't love them." This time, Victor did break down, and it was a few minutes before he was able to continue.

"Of course I loved them. They mean everything to me. But, you know, I searched through my mind and I couldn't recall a single time when I'd told them how much I loved them. Not one. The boys stayed together. They traveled around the world, stopping to work here and there, usually where there were surf beaches. Kathy went and saw them at different places over the years. They refused to accept any money from her. I gave her letters to give them, but they never replied.

"Then we started talking about the angels of abundance, and I realized I had everything, everything except what really mattered. You know I hadn't laughed, really laughed, in years. I did the ritual, and when I recited the Twenty-third Psalm I felt a sense of peace come over me. I hadn't read or said that Psalm in at least thirty years. I spoke to the angels, and they told me what to do." Victor paused and looked around the room. "That's why I haven't been here. I went to see my sons."

Victor almost choked up again. "Kathy told me where they were, and she promised not to tell them I was coming. They're in southern Thailand. They're doing very well." Victor smiled with pride. "They have a charter boat and take tourists out fishing. I booked a day on the boat. Actually, I booked the whole boat. You should have seen the look in the boys' faces when I turned up for the fishing trip. It was a bit awkward to begin with. We didn't do any fishing. We just sailed around in the boat and talked. We talked and talked. I finally managed to say what I should have said years and years ago. We hugged and cried. I spent the next two weeks with them, and they're coming home for Christmas. Kathy's already preparing for it. The funny thing is, I thought I was happy in the past, but I've never been happy, ever. I always thought making money was what it's all about, but I think I've finally learned what true abundance is all about."

Angels of Dreamtime

Many people call on the angels of dreamtime every night when they go to bed. It is a good practice to silently thank your guardian angel as you drift off to sleep.

When you were young, you might have learned a child's guardian angel poem:

> Matthew, Mark, Luke, and John,
> The bed be blest that I lie on.
> Four angels to my bed,
> Four angels round my head.
> One to watch and one to pray,
> And two to bear my soul away.

The first two lines of this verse are from *A Candle in the Dark* (1656) by Thomas Ady. It is not known if he wrote the entire verse.

I find it comforting and helpful to silently say this old verse to myself while falling asleep. It helps me relax and puts me in the right frame of mind for angelic contact in my dreams.

I like the childlike simplicity of Thomas Ady's poem, but some people feel too grown-up to use it. I suggest they use the Guardian Angel Prayer instead:

> Angel of God, my Guardian dear,
> To whom his love commits me here,
> Ever this day be at my side,

To light and guard, to rule and guide.

Amen.

Brenda's Experience

Brenda was in her late twenties when I first met her. She came to my classes because she was certain she had seen an angel. She was a good sleeper, but on this night she had woken up shortly after midnight. She went to the bathroom and returned to bed, confident that she'd fall asleep again in a matter of minutes. Half an hour later, she was wide awake and decided to read for a while, in the hope that doing so would send her to sleep. As she reached for the light switch, she sensed a presence and turned her head. Standing at the foot of her bed was an angel dressed entirely in white. Before she had a chance to react in any way, the vision disappeared. Brenda turned on the light and searched the room. She found no sign of an angel.

"I was starting to think I was seeing things," she told us. "But then I felt a sudden feeling of peace go right through me. I knew then that I'd really seen an angel, and he was looking after me."

Brenda enjoyed telling us each week about the exercises and rituals she'd performed. Initially, she was certain she'd see her angel again, but as each week passed without any sign of an angelic appearance, Brenda started to get discouraged.

"It's comforting to know he's there," she told us. "But he let me see him once. Why can't I see him again?"

Despite her growing concern about his non-appearance, Brenda wrote her guardian angel a letter and placed it under her pillow. She thanked him for his help, asked for an answer, and went to sleep.

She remembered her dream when she woke up the next day, but it had nothing to do with her question or her guardian angel. She wrote the letter again the following night and received no reply. When she came back to the class, she had written the letter six times.

"Even the problem doesn't seem like much anymore," she said. "I've thought about it every time I wrote the letter, and I know exactly what to do to resolve it."

"Maybe that's the message," one of the other students said. "Your guardian angel knows you know what to do. Why waste his time answering something you already know?"

"Fix the problem yourself," someone else said. "And then ask your guardian angel another question."

Brenda could see the wisdom in that, but as soon as she walked in a week later I could tell nothing had happened.

"Why is he doing this to me?" she asked. "I resolved the other problem, and wrote a new letter. He's ignoring it."

"Don't be too hasty," I told her. "Are you sure you haven't received an answer?"

Brenda frowned. "I think so. I thought about it as I wrote it, but then the next day I had the answer in my head, so didn't need to write it again."

"How did the answer pop into your head?"

Brenda laughed. "Oh, no! You don't think my guardian angel put it there, do you?"

After that, Brenda had no difficulty in communicating with her guardian angel by letter. She still hasn't seen him again, but knows she'll get an answer every time she writes to him.

Always contact your guardian angel if you have any doubts whatsoever about which angel you should contact. However, feel free to contact the other angels as well, even if it is simply to thank them for their love and care.

Conclusion

ngels seek to help and protect us at all times. I hope you'll continue to study angels, creating an ever closer connection and bond with them. Be alert to potential angelic connections wherever you go. Pay attention to your thoughts, intuitions, hunches, and dreams. Examine apparent coincidences and examples of serendipity to see if they've been helped by angelic intervention. Many times you will find they have.

Many people, myself included, have tried to dismiss the reality of angels. When I was working in a warehouse and started receiving messages from my guardian angel, my first thought was that I was becoming schizophrenic. I was reluctant to accept angels into my life then, but I am forever grateful that they insisted on establishing and maintaining contact. Thirty years later, when I was putting off writing another book on angels, I started finding small white feathers everywhere I went. Again the angels were encouraging me to do something I knew I should do.

The angels are talking to you, too. Remain receptive, listen, pray, practice the exercises in this book, perform the rituals, and welcome the angels into your life. They will deepen your connection with the divine and enhance your life in many different ways. You will become more intuitive, more aware, and more sensitive to the subtle nuances of everyday life. You will even look at rainbows and beautiful sunsets through different eyes. You will pay more attention to your dreams and discover your own inner wisdom. All of my students enhanced their lives as a result of communicating with angels. One of them transformed her life totally in a matter of days.

The pivotal moment of Lesley's entire life occurred when she was ten years old and almost drowned in the school swimming pool. She suffered from nightmares for many years afterward. Because of the terror she'd experienced in the swimming pool, she'd developed an incredible fear of death that kept her from sleeping at night. Every night, when Lesley went to bed, she'd wonder if she'd wake up in the morning. This fear made it hard for her to sleep. Communicating with her guardian angel removed those fears totally. Almost overnight, Lesley became more relaxed, confident, and sure of herself.

She was an exceptional case, but I saw positive changes in all my students. I know that contacting and communicating with the angelic kingdom has the potential to transform your life.

I wish you great success in your quest.

Dictionary of Angels

On the following pages are just a few of the tens of thousands of angels that have been named in the past. I have included as many of the positive and helpful angels as possible, as these are the ones who are most likely to be helpful to you.

ABARIEL Abariel is one of the regents of the moon and is often invoked in rituals involving emotions, fertility, childbirth, and female mysteries.

ABDIEL (or ABADIEL) During the War in Heaven, Abdiel refused to rebel against God and argued with Satan, saying that Satan had to be weaker than God, as God had created him. According to John Milton's *Paradise Lost*, Abdiel flew away, leaving Satan and his supporters behind. You should call on Abdiel in any matters concerning faith in yourself and faith in God.

ABULIEL Abuliel is one of several angels who specialize in carrying prayers to the Throne of God. The others are Akatriel, Metatron, Michael, Raphael, and Sizouse. Any of these angels can be invoked if you are sending a desperate prayer for help.

ACHAIAH Achaiah helps people become more patient and accepting.

ADIMUS Before 745 CE, Adimus was venerated by the Catholic Church. However, in that year, Pope Zachary demoted Adimus, Raguel, Simiel, and Archangel Uriel because none of them were mentioned by name in the Bible.

ADNACHIEL Adnachiel is the angel of independence who looks after anyone involved in pioneering or adventurous activities. He also looks after Sagittarians and the month of November.

AEONS In Gnosticism, aeons are a special order of angels who emanated from the Godhead. Each aeon was able to create other aeons, but the divine essence possessed less and less power with each generation. The best-known aeon is SOPHIA, sometimes called Pistis Sophia. Aeons were considered spiritual beings until the sixth century when they were excluded from the nine choirs of angels by Dionysius the Areopagite.

AFRIEL Afriel has a special interest in young people and can be invoked in any matters relating to children or teenagers.

AKATRIEL Akatriel is the angel who proclaims divine mysteries. He is one of the supreme regents of the Seventh Heaven. Akatriel can be consulted whenever doubt or mystery surrounds a problem.

AKRIEL Akriel helps people who have problems with infertility. These include conception, sterility, and lack of libido.

AMASRAS Amasras is mentioned in the *Book of Enoch*. He enjoys helping people who work with the soil, such as gardeners and farmers. He can also be called upon to increase the potency of magic spells.

AMBRIEL Ambriel is the ruling angel of May. He can be invoked for any matters involving communication. He also assists people who are seeking new jobs or searching for more opportunities and responsibility.

AMITIEL Amitiel is the angel of truth. He can be called upon for help in any matters requiring honesty and integrity.

ANABIEL According to the Kabbalah, Anabiel can be called upon to cure stupidity.

ANAEL ("The Grace of God") Anael (sometimes known as Haniel, Hagiel, Hanael, or Anael) is the chief of both the order of principalities and virtues. He is also lord of Venus and ruler of the third heaven. As a result, he can be invoked for any matters concerning love, romance, affection, sexuality, peace, harmony, and inner peace. Because of his association with love and affection, he is probably the most frequently invoked angel of all. Anael is believed to have taken Enoch to heaven. Anael helps people who are engaged in creative pursuits, and he endeavors to create beauty wherever he goes. Anael helps people overcome shyness and gain confidence in themselves.

ANAHITA Anahita is one of the angels of fertility. Anahita can be invoked for help in any matters concerning fertility and pregnancy.

ANAUEL Anauel is the angel of prosperity. He can be invoked in any matters concerning money or finance.

ANGEL OF AIR *See* Chassan.

ANGEL OF EARTH *See* Phorlach.

ANGEL OF FIRE *See* Aral.

ANGEL OF THE LORD The angel of the Lord appeared many times in the Bible. There is some confusion as to whether or not this term refers to the same angel each time, or even if the angel of the Lord is God Himself. It is generally believed that the angel of the Lord who appeared to Moses in the burning bush was the Archangel Michael.

ANGEL OF LOVE. *See* Shekinah.

ANGEL OF PEACE According to the Testament of Benjamin, the angel of peace looks after and guides the soul of a good person when he or she dies. The angel of peace escorted Enoch on his tour of heaven (recorded in I Enoch).

ANPIEL According to Jewish lore, Anpiel is the angel who is responsible for looking after birds.

ARAL (or AREL) Aral is the angel of fire. The term "angel of fire" has been used to describe a number of angels. According to the Zohar, Archangel Gabriel visited Moses in a flame of fire. In Zoroastrianism, Atar is the angel of fire. Uriel is sometimes considered the angel of fire, as his name means "flame of God." Ardarel is sometimes referred to as the angel of fire, and Aral might be an abbreviation of Ardarel.

ARCHANGELS The prefix "arch-" means "chief, principal, or most important." Consequently, archangels are among the most important angels. According to the Book of Revelation, there are seven archangels, though other sources list four, six, or nine. The Koran recognizes four archangels, but names only two: Djibril (Gabriel) and Michael. Michael, Gabriel, Raphael, and Uriel are the best-known archangels. Other possible archangels include Anael, Metatron, Orifiel, Raguel, Raziel, Remiel, Saraqael, and Zadkiel.

ARIEL ("Lion of God") Ariel is mentioned in the pseudepigraphal *Book of Ezra* and *The Key of Solomon the King*. He is believed to help Raphael cure illness and disease in humans, animals, and plants.

ARMAITA Armaita can be invoked when it is important to determine the truth of a matter.

ARMISAEL Armisael is traditionally invoked in matters relating to labor and childbirth. Gabriel and Temeluch are invoked to help the child while it is in the womb, but it is Armisael who is responsible for the birth process.

ASARIEL Asariel is the lord of Neptune. He looks after people who are involved in clairvoyance and mediumship. He can also be invoked to help heal sick horses.

ASHMODIEL Ashmodiel is one of the regents of the sign of Taurus. He can be invoked on any matters involving love and romance.

AZRAEL ("Whom God Helps") Azrael lives in the third heaven, and has the monumental task of recording everybody's names when they are born, and erasing them again when they die. In Jewish and Islamic lore, he is considered the angel of death. This is probably because of his interest in reincarnation. He can be called upon when exploring past lives, or when investigating psychic topics.

BALTHIAL Balthial can be invoked to help in situations when you should forgive someone else but find it difficult to do so.

BARAKIEL (or BARACHIEL) ("God's Blessings") Barakiel is ruler of the seraphim, and governor of the month of February. He provides a positive outlook on life and good fortune. Gamblers desiring success with their wagers also invoke Barakiel.

BATH KOL (or BAT QOL) ("Heavenly Voice") According to ancient tradition, it was Bath Kol who was first to ask Cain where his brother was. He is also believed to have visited Rabbi Simeon ben Yohai, reputed author of the Zohar, while he was in prison. Bath Kol helps people engaged in prophecy. Diviners can call out Bath Kol's name to help understand an omen or intuition. The next words the diviner hears are believed to contain the answer.

BETHELDA Bethelda is the angel who appeared to Geoffrey Hodson, the clairvoyant and Theosophist, in 1924. Bethelda told him that angels were divided into specialized groups, such as the angels of healing and the angels of nature.

CAMAEL *See* Chamuel.

CASSIEL Cassiel is the lord of Saturn and the sign of Capricorn. He is also ruler of the seventh heaven. He helps people understand patience and encourages them to overcome longstanding obstacles and problems. He provides serenity and teaches temperance. Cassiel is associated with karma and helps people understand the law of cause and effect. Because of his association with Saturn, Cassiel works slowly. As it takes Saturn four years to orbit the sun, Cassiel can take up to four years to resolve a problem. Fortunately, Raphael is willing to talk with Cassiel to speed the process up.

CHAMUEL (or CAMAEL, CAMIEL, KEMUEL) ("He Who Sees God") Chamuel is head of the choir of dominions and is one of the seven great archangels. He can

be called upon for any matters involving tolerance, understanding, forgiveness, and love. Chamuel is also one of the
ten Kabbalistic archangels. He rights wrongs, soothes trou-
bled minds, and provides justice. Chamuel is ruler of Mars.
You should call on Chamuel whenever you need additional
strength, or are in conflict with someone else. Chamuel
provides courage, persistence, and determination.

CHASSAN is the angel of air.

CHERUBIM The cherubim are the second-highest rank of angels in Dionysius' hierarchy. They are God's record keepers
and reflect his wisdom and divine intelligence. They pay
careful attention to all the details.

DAYS OF THE WEEK Certain angels are associated with each
day of the week. *See* Planetary Angels.

DINA According to the Kabbalah, Dina is one of the guardians of the Torah, and has a special interest in learning and
wisdom.

DJIBRIL Djibril is the Islamic version of Archangel Gabriel.
Djibril is a huge angel. He has six hundred or more beautiful
green wings that cover most of the horizon. He has a shin-
ing face, with the words "There is no God but God, and
Muhammad is the Prophet of God" written between his
eyes. It was Djibril who dictated the Koran to Muhammad.

DOMINIONS The dominions are the fourth most important
rank of angels in Dionysius' hierarchy. They work in heav-
en as middle-level executives, deciding what needs to be

done and then issuing the necessary orders to ensure that the universe works the way it should.

DONQUEL Donquel is one of the angels of Venus. He can be invoked by men desiring the love of a good woman.

ECANUS Ecanus has a special interest in people involved in writing. He can be invoked by people intending to make a career in literary pursuits.

ELEMIAH According to the Kabbalah, Elemiah is one of the seraphs of the Tree of Life. Elemiah can be invoked by anyone involved in inner growth and spiritual pursuits.

ENOCH *See* Metatron.

ERELIM (or ARELIM) In Jewish mysticism, the erelim are huge angels who look after plants and vegetation. They observe what is happening in the natural world and report their findings directly to God. This is easy for them to do, as they apparently have seventy thousand heads, and each head has seventy thousand mouths. Each mouth has seventy thousand tongues, and each tongue has seventy thousand sayings.

ETH ("Time") Eth is the angel who ensures that everything happens at the correct time. Eth can be invoked for guidance and help when one's patience is exhausted.

EZGADI Ezgadi is one of the angels who can be invoked for protection while traveling.

GABRIEL ("God Is My Strength") Gabriel, one of the four named archangels in the Hebraic tradition, is the Angel of the Annunciation and God's main messenger. Gabriel is one of the three angels who are mentioned by name in the Bible. (The others are Michael and Raphael. Raphael figures in the *Book of Tobit*, part of the Roman Catholic Bible.) Gabriel is the ruler of the cherubim and sits on God's left-hand side. It was Gabriel who told the Virgin Mary that she would give birth to Christ. Muslims believe Gabriel dictated the Koran to Muhammad. Gabriel is the angel of purification, guidance, and prophecy.

GAVREEL Gavreel is one of the guardians of the second heaven. (Some authorities believe he looks after the fourth heaven.) Gavreel can provide inner peace when it is required.

GAZARDIEL Gazardiel is one of the angels responsible for the sunrise. Consequently, he can be invoked for a new start or new beginnings.

GUARDIAN ANGEL The concept of a guardian angel is extremely old. In Zoroastrianism, guardian angels were called *fravashis*. Before Christianity, the Romans had protective guardians. Men had a *genius* and women a *juno*. Jesus Christ confirmed the existence of guardian angels when he said: "Take heed that ye despise not one of these little ones; for I say unto you, That in heaven their angels do always behold the face of my Father which is in heaven" (Matthew 18:10). Origen, an early Christian theologian, believed that everyone has both a good and an evil angel. The good angel guides and protects the person, and the evil angel tempts him or her. Saint Thomas Aquinas believed everyone has a guardian angel. In Catholic belief, everyone receives a guardian angel at birth to look after and guide them through life. On October second every year, Catholics have a feast day to celebrate guardian angels. In the Jewish Talmud, it is said that every Jew has eleven thousand guardian angels. Muslims have four guardian angels, known as Hafaza. Two watch over their charges during the day, while the other two look after them at night. These four angels are kept busy writing down their charges' good and bad deeds. These records will be used to assess each person on Judgment Day. It is important to communicate with your guardian angel in good times as well as bad. Your guardian angel will provide you with peace of mind in times of sorrow and misfortune, and will fill you with good ideas, positivity, and a desire to do good in the happy times.

HAAMIAH Haamiah is the angel of integrity and traditionally looks after genuine seekers of spiritual knowledge.

HABBIEL Habbiel is associated with the first heaven and the moon. Habbiel has a strong interest in love, loyalty, and commitment. He is the angel to call on if you or your partner experience problems in committing yourselves to each other.

HADRANIEL ("Greatness of God") In Hebrew tradition, God rebuked Hadraniel as he made Moses weep when he arrived in heaven to receive the Torah. After this, Hadraniel decided to help Moses, and did this by using his powerful voice. Apparently, Hadraniel's voice can penetrate two hundred thousand firmaments. Each word he says produces twelve thousand flashes of lightning. You should call on Hadraniel whenever you need help to express yourself.

HAEL Hael is the angel to call upon when you wish to send blessings to someone to thank them for their help or kindness.

HAFAZA *See* Guardian Angel.

HAMAEL Hamael can be invoked whenever it is essential to appear calm and dignified. Hamael provides persistence, determination, and practicality.

HAMALIEL Hamaliel is one of the rulers of August and the sign of Virgo. Hamaliel can be invoked for any matters involving logic and attention to detail.

HANIEL *See* Anael.

HARAHEL (or HARAREL) Harahel is the angel responsible for libraries, archives, and other repositories of knowledge. He can be called upon for help and advice on any matters involving study and learning.

HAZIEL Haziel is a member of the choir of cherubim. He should be invoked whenever you are seeking God's mercy and compassion.

HODNIEL Hodniel is one of the angels who can be called upon to help cure human stupidity.

IAHHEL Iahhel looks after the needs of hermits and philosophers. He can be invoked for help in meditation and for counsel during periods of self-imposed retirement from the world.

IOFIEL *See* Jophiel.

ISDA Isda is the angel who provides mankind with spiritual nourishment. He can be invoked by anyone desiring spiritual sustenance.

ITQAL Itqal works with Archangel Haniel and specializes in resolving disagreements, especially between family members. Itqal also restores love and affection and enhances consideration of others.

JEGUDIEL ("The Glory of God") The Archangel Jegudiel helps anyone who is attempting a closer relationship with God. He provides opportunities for people who are honest, sincere, and prepared to work hard to achieve worthwhile spiritual goals.

JEHOEL Jehoel is the ruler of the order of seraphim. According to the Apocalypse of Abraham, Jehoel took Abraham on a tour of heaven and ultimately took him to meet God. In Jewish legend, Jehoel leads the heavenly choirs that ceaselessly sing God's praises. Jehoel is happy to help musicians, especially singers.

JELIAL (or JELIEL) Jelial belongs to the order of seraphim. Members of this choir do not normally assist people, as they are engrossed in serving God. However, Jelial has always had an interest in stimulating love and passion inside existing relationships. You should call on Jelial if your relationship is suffering from a lack of passion.

JEREMIEL Archangel Jeremiel is mentioned in the Book of Esdras. It is possible that Jeremiel is another name for Archangel Uriel.

JOPHIEL (or IOPHIEL, IOFIEL, or ZOPHIEL) ("The Beauty of God") Jophiel is believed to have guarded the Tree of Knowledge in the Garden of Eden. He also looked after Noah's three sons. Jophiel is one of the princes of the Divine Presence and is believed to be a close friend of Metatron. He has a strong interest in beauty and can be invoked by anyone involved in creating beauty in any form. Jophiel helps people who are using their creativity. You should call on him whenever you need help with a creative project.

KAKABEL (or KOCHBIEL) ("Star of God") Kakabel is a controversial angel who performs the honorable task of looking after the moon and stars. However, according to some accounts, he lost his reputation by teaching humans astrology. Even worse, he was accused of mating with human women. Despite this, he still looks after astrologers as well as the stars and their formations.

KERUBIEL One of the leaders of the cherubim. His height spans all seven heavens and powerful flames come out of his mouth with every word he speaks. His body consists of burning coals covered with thousands of piercing eyes. Thunder, lightning, and earthquakes accompany him everywhere he goes. Despite his threatening appearance, he glows with the divine light of the Shekinah.

LAHABIEL Lahabiel is one of Raphael's chief assistants. He can be invoked to ward off evil of any sort. Traditionally, Lahabiel was invoked to protect people from magic spells, curses, or the evil eye. However, he can also be invoked whenever you see evil in any form.

LAILAH Lailah is the Jewish angel of night. Whenever a woman conceives, Lailah takes the sperm to God, who then decides what sort of person the resulting child will become. After this, God orders a soul to enter the embryo, and an angel stands guard to prevent it from escaping. Lailah looks after all matters relating to conception and pregnancy.

LIBERATING ANGEL This is how the Shekinah was described in the Kabbalah. *See* Shekinah.

LIWET Liwet is an angel of creativity who can be called upon when you have doubts about your creative abilities.

MACHIDIEL Machidiel is one of the angels of the Tree of Life. He can be invoked by men seeking love.

MAION Maion is the angel to invoke whenever you need self-control or self-discipline.

MALAHIDAEL Malahidael can be invoked whenever you need the necessary courage to stand up for what you believe is right.

MEHIEL According to Jewish mysticism, Mehiel looks after writers, teachers, and communicators.

MELCHIZEDEK (or MELCHISEDEK) Melchizedek belongs to the order of principalities and virtues. Dionysius the Areopagite wrote that he was the hierarch most loved and favored by God. Saint Hippolytus (c. 170–235), the Christian leader and antipope, considered Melchizedek to be more important than Jesus Christ. In the *Book of Mormon*, Melchizedek is the prince of peace. Melchizedek can be called upon when you need peace, tranquillity, and the love of God.

METATRON Metatron is chancellor of heaven and one of the leaders of the seraphim. Metatron is the most important angel in Jewish lore, which probably accounts for his name, which means "the throne beside the Throne of God." According to legend, Metatron was originally Enoch, a man who lived for three hundred and sixty-five years on earth before "God took him" and turned him into an angel (Genesis 5:23–24). Metatron, the angel, has three hundred and sixty-five thousand eyes and thirty-six wings. Enoch had been a scribe before his transformation and has continued working as God's secretary. In Jewish belief, Metatron carries Jewish prayers through nine hundred heavens directly to God. According to the Zohar, Metatron combines both human and angelic perfection, and this serves him in good stead in his role of ruling the entire world. Fortunately, he has seventy angelic princes to help him in this work. You should call on Metatron whenever you are engaged in deep thought.

MICHAEL ("Who Is Like God") The Archangel Michael is the greatest angel in Christianity, Islam, and Judaism. This is not surprising, as Michael is God's most important warrior angel, who fights for everything that is good, honorable, and righteous. Michael is ruler of the order of principalities and virtues, chief of the archangels, prince of the Presence, and angel of repentance. Michael threw Satan out of heaven after the battle between the good and evil angels. Michael also has the task of accompanying souls back to heaven after physical death. Michael is often shown carrying scales, as he has the important task of weighing souls to determine their worthiness at the Last Judgment.

MIHAEL According to the Kabbalah, Mihael is the angel of fertility. Mihael can also be invoked to ensure loyalty and faithfulness.

MONTHLY ANGELS These are the angels that govern each month of the year:

> January: Gabriel or Cambiel
> February: Barchiel
> March: Machidiel or Malahidael
> April: Asmodel
> May: Ambriel
> June: Muriel
> July: Verchiel
> August: Hamaliel
> September: Uriel or Zuriel
> October: Barbiel
> November: Adnachiel or Advachiel
> December: Anael

MORONI Moroni is the angel who appeared to Joseph Smith, founder of the Church of Jesus Christ of Latter-day Saints, and told him where to dig up the golden plates that contained the *Book of Mormon*.

MURIEL Muriel is one of the regents of the choir of dominions. He is also responsible for the sign of Cancer and looks after the month of July. Muriel can be invoked whenever your emotions need to be kept under control.

NEMAMIAH Nemamiah belongs to the choir of archangels and has a strong interest in just causes. You should invoke Nemamiah whenever you are seeking justice.

OPHANIEL One of the leaders of the cherubim.

PASCHAR Seven angels, including Paschar, stand in front of the Holy Throne. He can be called upon if you are seeking help in prophecy or divination.

PERPETIEL Perpetiel can be invoked if you are working on a worthwhile project, but are finding it hard to accomplish. Perpetiel will help you achieve success.

PHANUEL *See* Raguel.

PHORLACH (or FORLAC) Angel of earth.

PLANETARY ANGELS The ancient Romans associated the days of the week with the seven visible planets. This association gradually took on more and more elements, including angels. The first documented evidence of this comes from twelfth-century Spain. Esoteric philosophy flourished at that time, and European scholars began translating valuable books from the past, discovering many insights in the process. Here are the planets and angels that are generally associated with each day of the week:

Sunday: Sun—Michael
Monday: Moon—Gabriel
Tuesday: Mars—Camael
Wednesday: Mercury—Raphael
Thursday: Jupiter—Sachiel
Friday: Venus—Anael
Saturday: Saturn—Cassiel

POWERS The powers are the sixth-highest rank of angels, according to Dionysius. Their task is to ensure that all the laws of the universe work perfectly.

PRINCIPALITIES The principalities are the seventh-highest ranked angels in Dionysius' hierarchy. They guide and assist leaders, rulers, and nations. They also assist religions in spreading the truth and supervise the rise and fall of nations.

RAGUEL ("Friend of God") Raguel, sometimes known as Phanuel, supervises the behavior of his fellow angels, and is ruler of the order of dominions. Some people believe it was Raguel who brought Enoch to heaven. Raguel is considered a kind, caring assistant to God. You should call on Raguel if you are trying to affirm or strengthen your faith.

RAHMIEL (or RHAMIEL) Rahmiel and Raphael are the two angels of compassion. Rahmiel can be called upon to help people who lack love and compassion. Some people believe that when Saint Francis died, he became the angel Rahmiel. Enoch and Elijah are the only other humans who may have been transformed into angels.

RAPHAEL ("God heals") Raphael is one of the most important archangels. Raphael is considered regent of the sun, ruler of the second heaven, and chief of the order of principalities and virtues. He has a special interest in healing, creativity, knowledge, science, communication, travel, and young people. Raphael has been considered a guardian angel since he acted as Tobias's guardian in the *Book of Tobit*. He also looks after the guardian angels. In effect, Raphael is the guardian angel of humanity.

RAZIEL ("Secret of God") Raziel is the wise angel who felt sorry for Adam and Eve when they were banished from the Garden of Eden. He gave Adam the *Book of the Angel Raziel*. This book contained all the knowledge of the universe and enabled Adam to make a life for himself outside the Garden. After Adam's death, the book was eventually found by Enoch (see Metatron), who memorized it and became the wisest man of his time. Later still, it came into the hands of Noah, who used it to help build his ark. Hundreds of years later, the book belonged to King Solomon, who used it to create magic. Unfortunately, after his death, the book disappeared. You should contact Raziel whenever you need answers to imponderable questions. Raziel particularly enjoys helping original thinkers develop their ideas.

REHAEL Rehael belongs to the choir of powers, and is the angel of longevity. Rehael can be invoked for health matters, self-respect, and respect for others (especially parents).

REMIEL Remiel is the angel of divine vision. He is an archangel who has the task of looking after the souls of the faithful after they have been weighed by Michael. He is happy to help people with a particular need to see into the future.

ROCHEL Rochel is the angel of lost property and can be invoked when anything is misplaced or lost.

RUBIEL Rubiel is known as the gamblers' friend and can be invoked whenever you are playing games of chance.

SACHIEL Sachiel is considered the lord of Jupiter and is a member of the choir of cherubim. He has an interest in legal matters, good fortune, expansion, and beneficence. He is often invoked on financial matters. Sachiel is willing to help you earn money, but will not help you obtain money for nothing.

SAGNESSAGIEL Sagnessagiel is the prince of wisdom. He provides wisdom, knowledge, and understanding. He teaches patience and forgiveness. It is possible that Sagnessagiel is another name for Metatron.

SALAPHIEL ("Communicant of God") Salaphiel is listed as one of the seven main archangels in the *Book of Tobit* and the Book of Esdras. Salaphiel's main task is to help people pray. You should call on him for help if you find yourself easily distracted while praying, and if you want to learn how to pray more effectively.

SAMANDIRIEL Samandiriel is the angel of fertility. Anyone having problems with conception can invoke Samandiriel and ask for help. Samandiriel can also be called upon on for any matter concerning imagination, visualization, and creativity.

SAMAEL Samael was originally considered an evil angel in Judaism. Samael means "blind god." In this sense, "blind" means ignorant, and the Gnostics considered ignorance to be the seat of evil. Today, Samael is considered a protective angel who provides persistence and courage whenever necessary. Samael is willing to help us deal with our enemies in a gentle manner, to defuse and eliminate long-lasting difficulties.

SANDALPHON (or SANDALFON) Sandalphon helps Metatron weave Jewish prayers into garlands for God to wear on his head. Despite his preference for Jewish prayers, Sandalphon is willing to carry any prayer to heaven. According to Jewish legend, Sandalphon was originally the prophet Elijah and is considered Metatron's twin brother. According to the Bible, "Elijah went up by a whirlwind into heaven" (2 Kings 2:11). Sandalphon is extremely tall, and it is believed that it would take five hundred years to climb from his feet to the top of his head.

SARIEL ("God's Command") According to the *Book of Enoch*, Sariel was one of the original seven archangels. Sariel helps people who want to learn. In Hebrew lore, Sariel encouraged Moses to study. He is also interested in healing and assists Raphael in this work. Sariel provides guidance whenever it is needed. Sariel is frequently invoked in ceremonial magic and provides protection against the evil eye.

SEASONAL ANGELS The seasonal angels govern the four seasons:

> Spring: Amatiel, Caracasa, Core, and Commissoros
> Summer: Gargatel, Gaviel, and Tariel
> Autumn: Tarquam and Guabarel
> Winter: Amabael and Ceterari

SEDEKIAH Sedekiah is frequently invoked by prospectors and people searching for hidden treasure, such as gold and diamonds.

SERAPHIEL (or SERAPIEL) Seraphiel is one of the leaders of the seraphim. Saint Francis is one of the few humans to have seen a seraph. You cannot invoke a seraph, but you can ask Seraphiel to provide you with peace of mind.

SERAPHIM ("The Burning Ones") The seraphim are the highest-ranking of the nine choirs of angels, and are the angels closest to God. They have four faces and six wings. Their light is so strong that humans could not exist in their presence. The seraphim fly endlessly around the celestial throne singing, "Holy, holy, holy."

SEVEN HEAVENS, ANGELS OF Christians, Jews, and Muslims all believe in heaven. Apocalyptic accounts of heaven range from one heaven to ten, but most agree on seven, probably because of the seven visible planets. The tradition of seven heavens probably originated in Mesopotamia seven thousand years ago.

FIRST HEAVEN—The first heaven contains the physical world. It is ruled by Gabriel and is home to all the angels connected with the natural phenomena of the universe.

SECOND HEAVEN—The second heaven is ruled by Raphael. It is the home of sinners who are waiting for Judgment Day. Some of the fallen angels are held here.

THIRD HEAVEN—Baradiel is in charge of the third heaven. The southern half of this heaven contains the Garden of Eden and the Tree of Life. Three hundred angels of light protect them. The northern half of the third heaven could not be more different, as it contains hell. Not surprisingly, some of the fallen angels are held here.

FOURTH HEAVEN—The fourth heaven is ruled by Michael. It contains the holy Temple and the Altar of God.

FIFTH HEAVEN—Most sources say that Zadkiel rules the fifth heaven. (Some accounts give this task to Sandalphon.) Some of the fallen angels are held here (as well as in the second and third heavens).

SIXTH HEAVEN—Zebul rules the sixth heaven at night, and Sabath rules during the daytime hours. All the celestial records are kept here, and choirs of angels endlessly study them.

SEVENTH HEAVEN—Archangel Cassiel rules the seventh heaven. God, the seraphim, cherubim, and thrones live here.

SHAMSHIEL ("Light of Day") According to Jewish tradition, Shamshiel looks after the Garden of Eden. He gave Moses a guided tour of the Garden. He is prepared to help everyone who has a genuine desire to improve their garden.

SHEKINAH, THE In Jewish tradition, the Shekinah is the feminine aspect of God. *Shekinah* means "shelter" or "dwelling place." She is the Great Mother of the universe, the Queen of Heaven. She is believed to be the angel Jacob referred to as "the angel which redeemed me from all evil" (Genesis 48:16). Jewish mystics tell how the Shekinah was separated from her lover, God the Father, after Adam and Eve were expelled from the Garden of Eden. Ever since then, they have been together only on Friday nights, the night before the Sabbath. They will be finally reunited only when the original light of Creation returns to its source. Fortunately, every act of love, generosity, and compassion brings the couple closer together. The Shekinah provides unity and peace of mind. She delights in helping all lovers.

SOPHIA ("Wisdom") Sophia is one of the most important aeons. Some people consider Sophia to be the greatest of all angels, as they believe she gave birth to all the other angels.

TAHARIEL Tahariel is the angel of chastity and purification. Tahariel is the angel to call on when you need a respite from everyday relationships and seek a greater association with the Divine. This time can be short or long, but it will purify your body, mind, heart, and soul.

TEIAZEL Teiazel is the angel who looks after writers, artists, sculptors, and musicians. He can be invoked by these people whenever they need help in their creative activities.

TEMELUCH Temeluch is responsible for pregnancy and traditionally assists Gabriel in instructing the unborn child before it is born.

TEOAEL Teoael is a member of the choir of thrones. He can be invoked to help new business ventures. Traditionally, he was invoked to protect ships heading out to sea with precious cargoes. The best way to call on Teoael is to write him a letter explaining exactly what you desire. Send it to him using the ritual in chapter 3.

TEZALEL Tezalel is the angel responsible for trust and fidelity in all loving relationships. You should call on Tezalel if you have any concerns about the quality of your relationship.

THELIEL Thelial is the angelic prince of love. Not surprisingly, he is associated with the planet Venus. You should call on him if you want to attract love into your life. Thelial will not make a specific person fall in love with you, as this might not be in the best interest of both parties. However, he will create situations in which you can meet people who are suitable candidates.

THRONES The thrones are the third-highest ranking of angels. They are sometimes called "wheels," as Ezekiel, the Old Testament prophet, saw them as fiery wheels. They are angels of justice. Their task is to advise God when he makes important decisions.

URIEL ("Fire of God") Uriel is the archangel of prophecy. He is also regent of the sun and in charge of all natural phenomena, such as floods and earthquakes. In Jewish legend, Uriel warned Noah of the imminent flood. He is also the overseer of hell. Uriel can be called upon to help with creative activities.

UZZIEL ("God's Power") Uzziel provides faith and hope in our darkest moments. Uzziel is the angel to invoke when everything seems hopeless and there seems no point in carrying on.

VALOEL Valoel provides peace, contentment, and understanding. When life is overly hectic or tumultuous, Valoel can provide the necessary peace of mind to handle the situation.

VASIARIAH Vasiariah belongs to the choir of dominions and looks after lawyers, judges, and courts of law. He can be invoked in any matters concerning justice, honesty, and fairness.

VERCHIEL (or VARCHIEL) Verchiel is one of the regents of the choir of powers. He provides love, affection, and friendship. You should call on Verchiel when you are experiencing difficulties with family or good friends.

VIRTUES The virtues are the fifth-highest rank of angels in Dionysius' hierarchy. They are in charge of all natural laws to keep the universe working as it should. Because of this, they are also responsible for miracles that go against these laws. Archangel Michael is prince regent of the choir of virtues. The other regents include Barbiel, Peliel, Raphael, and Uzziel.

VRETIL Vretil is the divine scribe who looks after the sacred books in heaven. He is believed to be the wisest angel of all. Vretil can be invoked whenever you seek wisdom or insight.

YEHUDIAH Yehudiah is the angel of bereavement and can be called upon for comfort when a loved one dies. He is one of God's chief messengers.

ZACHARIEL Zachariel can be invoked to help people improve their memory.

ZADKIEL or TZADKIEL ("Righteousness of God") Zadkiel is the ruler of Jupiter, regent of Sagittarius, and is believed to be chief of the choir of dominions. Zadkiel is also the angel of divine justice. Because of his association with Jupiter, Zadkiel provides abundance, benevolence, mercy, forgiveness, tolerance, compassion, prosperity, happiness, and good fortune. According to Jewish legend, it was Zadkiel who prevented Abraham from sacrificing his son Isaac. You should call on Zadkiel for help whenever you experience financial or legal problems.

ZAGZAGEL ("God's Righteousness") In Hebrew lore, Zagzagel is the angel of the burning bush who gave advice to Moses (Exodus 3:2). Zagzagel advised and taught Moses, and was one of the three angels who escorted his soul to heaven. Zagzagel is believed to rule the fourth heaven. In his spare time, he also teaches other angels. You should call on Zagzagel whenever you need knowledge or wisdom.

ZODIAC, ANGELS OF THE Angels have been associated with the twelve signs of the zodiac for thousands of years. It is a logical association as angels, stars, and planets are all associated with the celestial realms. Here are the traditional associations of angels with the astrological signs:

Aries: Malahidael or Machidiel

Taurus: Asmodel

Gemini: Ambriel

Cancer: Muriel

Leo: Verchiel

Virgo: Hamaliel

Libra: Uriel or Zuriel

Scorpio: Barbiel

Sagittarius: Advachiel or Adnachiel

Capricorn: Hanael

Aquarius: Cambiel or Gabriel

Pisces: Barchiel

ZURIEL Zuriel is the prince regent of the choir of principalities. He also looks after the sign of Libra and is ruler of September. Zuriel can be invoked to create harmony and accord.

Suggested Reading

Auerbach, Loyd. *Psychic Dreaming: A Parapsychologist's Handbook*. New York: Warner Books, 1991.

Bailey, Foster. *Changing Esoteric Values*. Tunbridge Wells, UK: The Lucis Press, 1954.

Brown, Michael H. *The Trumpet of Gabriel*. Milford, OH: Faith Publishing, 1994.

Bunson, Matthew. *Angels A to Z: A Who's Who of the Heavenly Host*. New York: Three Rivers Press, 1996.

Chase, Steven (translator). *Angelic Spirituality: Medieval Perspectives on the Ways of Angels*. New York: Paulist Press, 2002.

Cunningham, Scott. *Dreaming the Divine: Techniques for Sacred Sleep.* St. Paul, MN: Llewellyn, 1999.

Finley, Guy. *The Lost Secrets of Prayer: Practices for Self-Awakening.* St. Paul, MN: Llewellyn, 1998.

Gackenbach, Jayne and Jane Bosveld. *Control Your Dreams: How Lucid Dreaming Can Help You Uncover Your Hidden Desires, Confront Your Hidden Fears, and Explore the Frontiers of Human Consciousness.* New York: Harper and Row, 1989.

Giovetti, Paola. *Angels: The Role of Celestial Guardians and Beings of Light,* trans. Toby McCormick. York Beach, ME: Samuel Weiser, 1993. (Originally published by Edizioni Mediterranee, Rome, Italy, 1989.)

Guiley, Rosemary Ellen. *Encyclopedia of Angels.* New York: Facts on File, 1996.

Hodson, Geoffrey. *The Brotherhood of Angels and Men.* Wheaton, IL: The Theosophical Publishing House, 1982. (Originally published in 1927.)

Hodson, Geoffrey. *The Kingdom of the Gods.* Adyar, India: The Theosophical Publishing House, 1952.

Jovanovic, Pierre. *An Inquiry into the Existence of Guardian Angels: A Journalist's Investigative Report.* New York: M. Evans, 1995.

Lewis, James R. and Evelyn Dorothy Oliver. *Angels A to Z.* Canton, MI: Visible Ink Press, 1996.

McCabe, Herbert. *God Still Matters.* London: Continuum, 2005.

MacGregor, Geddes. *Angels: Ministers of Grace.* New York: Paragon House, 1988.

Pennington, M. Basil. *Centering Prayer: Renewing an Ancient Christian Prayer Form.* New York: Image Books, 1982.

Ronner, John. *Know Your Angels: The Angel Almanac with Biographies of 100 Prominent Angels in Legend and Folklore, and Much More.* Murfreesboro, TN: Mamre Press, 1993.

Roth, Ron and Peter Occhiogrosso. *The Healing Path of Prayer: A Modern Mystic's Guide to Spiritual Power.* New York: Harmony Books, 1997.

Russell, Jeffrey Burton. *A History of Heaven: The Singing Silence.* Princeton, NJ: Princeton University Press, 1997.

Sanders, J. Oswald. *Prayer Power Unlimited.* Chicago: Moody Press, 1988.

Steere, Douglas V. *Dimensions of Prayer: Cultivating a Relationship with God* (revised edition). Nashville, TN: Upper Room Books, 1997. (Originally published in 1962.)

Webster, Richard. *Pendulum Magic for Beginners: Power to Achieve All Goals.* St. Paul, MN: Llewellyn, 2002.

Webster, Richard. *Spirit Guides and Angel Guardians: Contact Your Invisible Helpers.* St. Paul, MN: Llewellyn, 1998.

Webster, Richard. *Michael: Communicating with the Archangel for Guidance and Protection.* St. Paul, MN: Llewellyn, 2004.

Webster, Richard. *Raphael: Communicating with the Archangel for Healing and Creativity.* St. Paul, MN: Llewellyn, 2005.

Webster, Richard. *Gabriel: Communicating with the Archangel for Inspiration and Reconciliation.* St. Paul, MN: Llewellyn, 2005.

Webster, Richard. *Uriel: Communicating with the Archangel for Transformation and Tranquility.* Woodbury, MN: Llewellyn, 2005.

Index

Summoning the Fates

A Guide to Destiny and Sacred Transformation

ZSUZSANNA E. BUDAPEST

During the 1956 Hungarian Revolution, Z. Budapest narrowly escaped a massacre. Was it chance that spared her life, or destiny?

Budapest, a pioneer of the women's spirituality movement, introduces us to the three Fates that rule our lives. Not even the gods and goddesses can escape these raw forces of nature presiding over the past, present, and future. Budapest uses fairy tales, historical lore, and personal anecdotes to describe the three sacred sisters who are especially active during our thirty-year life cycles: Urdh (youth), Verdandi (adulthood), and Skuld (the crone years).

Want a taste of the cosmic soup bubbling in Fate's cauldron? Budapest also offers heartfelt advice, exercises, and rituals to help you connect with the Fates and embrace your own unique destiny.

0-7387-1083-0 / EAN 9780738710839

6 x 9   US $15.95 CAN $17.50

288 pp

bibliog

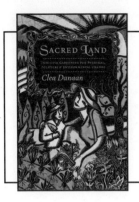

Sacred Land

Intuitive Gardening for Personal, Political, and Environmental Change

CLEA DANAAN

Clea Danaan breaks new ground with Sacred Land—a fresh approach to sacred gardening that goes beyond the backyard.

Danaan shows how the garden can germinate environmental awareness and political change while feeding the spirit. You'll learn how to create compost, save seeds, connect with garden goddesses, perform rituals and magic, and incorporate planetary energy in the garden. Each of the four sections—spanning earth, air, fire, and water—suggest ways of spreading this message of ecology and sustainability to the community. There are also inspiring stories of activists, farmers, artists, healers and other women who are making a difference in the world.

0-7387-1146-2 / EAN 9780738711461

5³⁄₁₆ x 8   US $15.95 CAN $17.50

336 pp

appendix, bibliog

Creative Visualization for Beginners

*Achieve Your Goals & Make Your Dreams
Come True*

RICHARD WEBSTER

Everyone has the natural ability to visualize success, but ordinary methods used to reach fulfillment can be inefficient and unclear. Creative
visualization allows anyone to change the direction of his or her life
by mentally picturing and altering images of their goals. In his popular conversational style, bestselling author Richard Webster explains the
methodology behind creative visualization, and provides readers with the
tools and knowledge necessary to achieve their goals in all areas of life,
including business, health, self-improvement, relationships, and nurtur-
ing and restoring the soul.

    Creative Visualization for Beginners includes simple exercises enhanced by real-
life situations from the author's personal experiences with creative visualization, and demonstrates how to react when you encounter difficulties along
the way. In addition, he gives advice on what to do if you have no predeter-
mined goals in mind, and how to implement positive results while maintaining your natural balance.

0-7387-0807-0 / EAN 9780738708072

5³⁄₁₆ x 8   US $12.95 CAN $17.50

264 pp

notes, index

Raphael

Communicating with the
Archangel for Healing & Creativity

RICHARD WEBSTER

A social worker finds sudden relief from a mysterious illness. A confused student discovers her true passion. A guilt-ridden widow reconnects with her daughter. These and other true stories, recounted by Richard Webster in *Raphael*, demonstrate the positive, healing impact this wise and benevolent archangel has had on countless lives.

Whether your pain is physical or emotional, the archangel Raphael—also known as the Divine Physician—can help. This book offers meditations, rituals, visualizations, amulets, and other practical techniques for contacting the "guardian angel of all humanity." Raphael can assist with health problems, finding lost or stolen items, emotional trauma, travel, spiritual guidance, and learning.

0-7387-0649-3 / EAN 9780738706498

US $11.95   CAN $12.95

5³⁄₁₆ x 8
192 pp.